# THE KNITTER'S ACTIVITY BOOK

This book belongs to

Name ..................................................... Age ............

Address ...................................................................

.............................................................................

**COLLINS & BROWN**

First published in the United Kingdom in 2019 by
Collins & Brown
43 Great Ormond Street
London
WC1N 3HZ

An imprint of Pavilion Books Company Ltd

Senior graphic designers: Peter Butler and Alastair Parr
Illustrations and set design by Octavia O'Donovan
Story concepts by Eleanor Flynn and Louise Walker

Distributed in the United States and Canada by
Sterling Publishing Co., Inc. 1166 Avenue of the Americas, New York, NY 10036

ISBN 978-1-91116-359-6

A CIP catalogue record for this book is available from the British Library.

10 9 8 7 6 5 4 3 2 1

Reproduction by Rival Colour Ltd, UK
Printed and bound in China by 1010 Printing International Limited

www.pavilionbooks.com

PUBLISHER'S NOTE: The author and publisher have made every effort to ensure that all instructions in the book are accurate and safe, and therefore cannot liability for any resulting injury , damage or loss to persons or property, however it may arise. It is the responsibility of the reader to ensure that any toys, clothes or accessories made using these patterns are safe for young children.

# The Knit List

# Welcome to *The Knitter's Activity Book*, a collection of twenty patterns celebrating fun and alternative knits.

I wanted to create something that was more than just a pattern book. Inspired by vintage annuals, I started working on this project. The result is this big colourful book, full of patterns, stories, puzzles, quizzes and more.

I hope you like it and that it keeps you busy for a long time. I can't wait to see all of your finished knits!

*Sincerely Louise*

# Abbreviations and Information

## TENSION (GAUGE)

The patterns in this book have various tensions. Please swatch before starting all projects and adjust your tension accordingly.

## CASTING ON

For all patterns either use the long-tail cast-on method, which creates the first row of knitting, or use the two-needle method and knit the first row. All patterns in this book begIn from **Row 2**, which is a purl row.

## COLOURS

**M** refers to the Main Colour, which will usually be the dominant colour. **C** refers to the Contrast Colour, which will be the other colour used in the pattern. Some patterns may use additional lettering for the other colours, such as A, B, etc.
*Example: K10M, K2C, K10M would mean knit 10 stitches in main colour, knit 2 stitches in contrast colour, knit 10 stitches in main colour.*

## COLOUR CHANGING

Either carry the yarns across the back of the work or use the intarsia technique (use a separate ball of yarn for each area of colour and twist the yarns around each other at each colour change to avoid holes). Some patterns state a preferred technique. For any patterns that do not, carry the yarn.

## ABBREVIATIONS

**B** Bobble stitch:
*Kfbf (3 sts), TURN*
*P the three stitches, TURN*
*Kfb three times (6 sts), TURN*
*K2tog three times (3 sts), TURN*
*K3tog (1 st) and continue working the piece*

**K** Knit

**K2tog** Knit two stitches together

**K3tog** Knit three stitches together

**Kfb** Knit into the front and back of the same stitch, increasing from one to two stitches

**Kfbf** Knit into the front, back and front again of the same stitch, increasing from one to three stitches

**L** Loop stitch; see the tutorial on page 11 for further details

**P** Purl

**SKP** Slip a stitch, knit a stitch, pass the slipped stitch over

**St st** Stocking (stockinette) stitch: knit a row, purl a row if working flat; if working in the round, knit every round

**TURN** Turn the work

**WA** Wrap around; this technique is used when knitting short rows

**Wrong side** The purl side of the knit

**\* \*** Repeat the instructions within the asterisks the number of times stated

## SCRAP YARN MARKERS

Some projects call for the use of scrap yarn markers to mark certain stitches. Use a small amount of scrap yarn or alternatively use stitch markers.

# GET SINCERELY LOUISE

BASED ON TRUE EVENTS

| 51 | **MOTORWAY DIVERSION** **52** GO BACK TO 44 | 53 |

| 50 |

| 49 | 48 | 47 |

| **STUCK IN TRAFFIC** **25** MISS A TURN | 26 | 27 |

| 24 |

| 18 | ↑ SET UP ANOTHER FAIR **19** DIVERSION | 20 | 21 | **REPLACE CAT CONVERTER** **22** GO BACK TO 20 | 23 |

| **FORGOT SOMETHING** **17** GO BACK TO START |

| 16 | 15 | 14 | 13 | 12 | 11 | **FLAT TYRE** **10** MISS A TURN | 9 |

# TO THE CRAFT FAIR

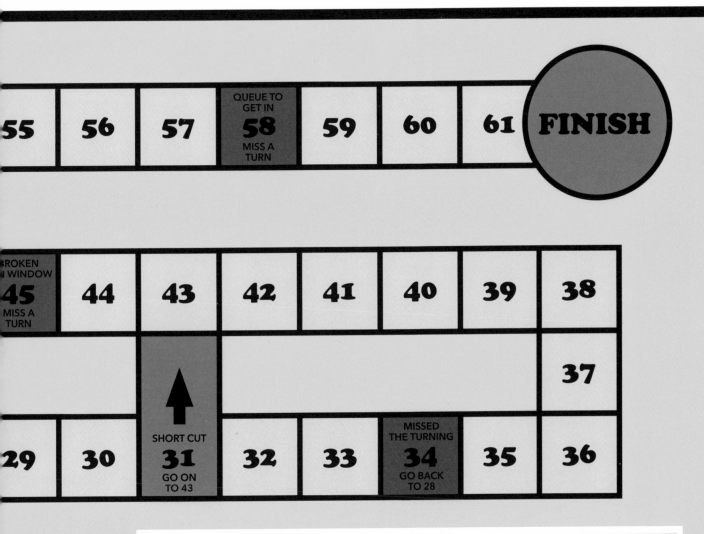

| 55 | 56 | 57 | QUEUE TO GET IN **58** MISS A TURN | 59 | 60 | 61 | **FINISH** |

| BROKEN WINDOW **45** MISS A TURN | 44 | 43 | 42 | 41 | 40 | 39 | 38 |

| | | SHORT CUT **31** GO ON TO 43 | | | | | 37 |

| 29 | 30 | SHORT CUT **31** GO ON TO 43 | 32 | 33 | MISSED THE TURNING **34** GO BACK TO 28 | 35 | 36 |

The Sincerely Louise team needs your help getting to the craft fair as things are always going wrong. Play using different-coloured counters and a dice. The player with the highest roll goes first. The winner is the first to reach the finish line, but the exact number must be thrown to win. The events depicted in this game are based on true life.

| 7 | VAN WON'T START **6** MISS A TURN | 5 | LATE YARN DELIVERY **4** GO BACK TO START | 3 | 2 | 1 | **START** |

# GUARD YOUR TEA

SINCERELY LOUISE

# WITH A LION MUG RUG

# LION MUG RUG

## MATERIALS

Sincerely Louise How Does It Feel,
100% wool, 115m per 100g (126yd per 3½oz),
or any lightweight chunky (bulky) yarn
**M** - Yellow - Optimistic x 1 ball
**C** - Cream - Loved x 1 ball
**B** - Orange - Courageous x 1 ball

6mm (US 10) straight needles, stitch holder,
a handful of toy stuffing, dried lavender
(optional), black DK yarn for embroidery

**Tension (Gauge):** 16 sts x 20 rows = 10cm (4in)
**Finished Size:** 28 x 22 x 6cm (11 x 8¾ x 2½in)

---

**TOP PIECE** – Make One
Cast on 3 stitches in C.
**Row 2** P
**Row 3** *Kfb* all stitches (6 sts)
**Row 4** P
**Row 5** K1M, K4C, K1M
**Row 6** P2M, P2C, P2M
**Row 7** Work all stitches in M until otherwise stated. K
**Row 8** P
**Row 9** *Kfb, K1* all stitches (9 sts)
**Row 10** P
**Row 11** *Kfb, K2* all stitches (12 sts)
**Row 12** P
**Row 13** K
**Row 14** P
**Row 15** K4M, K1B, L2B, K1B, K4M (*See loop stitch tutorial, page 11, for the L stitch.*)
**Row 16** P4M, P4B, P4M
**Row 17** K1B, K3M, L4B, K3M, K1B
**Row 18** Work all stitches in B until otherwise stated. P
**Row 19** K1, L10, K1
**Row 20** P
**Row 21** K1, L10, K1
**Row 22** P
**Row 23** K1M, L1B, K2tog in B, L2B, K2tog in B, L2B, K2tog in M (9 sts) (*When changing colour use the intarsia technique; see page 5.*)
**Row 24** P1M, P7B, P1M
**Row 25** Cast on 9 stitches in M at the beginning of the row, K9M, Kfbf in M, Kfbf in M, L5B, Kfbf in M, Kfbf in M (26 sts)
**Row 26** Cast on 9 stitches in M at the beginning of the row, P16M, P3B, P16M (35 sts)
**Row 27** Kfb in M, K15M, L3B, K14M, Kfb in M, K1M (37 sts)
**Row 28** P18M, P1B, P18M
**Row 29** K18M, L1B, K18M

**Row 30** Work all stitches in M from here. P
**Row 31** K1, SKP, K to the last three stitches, K2tog, K1 (35 sts)
**Row 32** P
**Row 33** Cast (bind) off 10 stitches, K to the end of the row (25 sts)
**Row 34** Cast (bind) off 10 stitches, P to the end of the row (15 sts)
**Row 35** K
**Row 36** P all even rows from here unless otherwise stated. P rows have been <u>underlined</u>.
**Row 37** K
**Row 39** K
**Row 41** Kfb, Kfb, K to the last three stitches, Kfb, Kfb, K1 (19 sts)
**Row 43** Kfb, K to the last two stitches, Kfb, K1 (21 sts)
**Row 45** Kfb, K to the last two stitches, Kfb, K1 (23 sts)

*Right Leg*
**Row 47** Kfb, K7 (9 sts), TURN, placing the remaining 15 stitches on a holder to be worked later.
<u>**Row 48**</u> P the 9 stitches
**Row 49** Kfb, K5, K2tog, K1 (9 sts)
**Row 51** K
**Row 53** K1, SKP, K3, K2tog, K1 (7 sts)
**Row 55** K1, SKP, K1, K2tog, K1 (5 sts)
**Row 57** Cast (bind) off.

*Tail*
Move 7 stitches from the holder onto the left-hand needle ready to be worked from Row 47.
**Row 47** Reattach the yarn and K1, SKP, K1, K2tog, K1 (5 sts)
<u>**Row 48**</u> P the 5 stitches
**Row 49** K
**Row 51** K
**Row 53** K

**Row 55** K
**Row 57** Work all stitches in B from here. K1, L3, K1
**Row 59** K1, L3, K1.
Cut the yarn leaving a small tail, thread it through the remaining five stitches and pull tightly.

### *Left Leg*
Move 8 stitches from the holder onto the left-hand needle ready to be worked from Row 47.
**Row 47** Reattach the yarn and K6, Kfb, K1 (9 sts)
**Row 49** K1, SKP, K4, Kfb, K1 (9 sts)
**Row 51** K
**Row 53** K1, SKP, K3, K2tog, K1 (7 sts)
**Row 55** K1, SKP, K1, K2tog, K1 (5 sts)
**Row 57** Cast (bind) off.

### UNDER PIECE – Make One
Cast on 3 stitches in C.
**Row 2** P all even rows unless otherwise stated. P rows have been <u>underlined</u>.
**Row 3** *Kfb* all stitches (6 sts)
**Row 5** K1M, K4C, K1M
<u>**Row 6**</u> P2M, P2C, P2M
**Row 7** Work all stitches in M until otherwise stated. K
**Row 9** *Kfb, K1* all stitches (9 sts)
**Row 11** *Kfb, K2* all stitches (12 sts)
**Row 13** K
**Row 15** K
**Row 17** Work all stitches in B until otherwise stated. K1, L10, K1
**Row 19** K1, L10, K1
**Row 21** K1, L10, K1
**Row 23** Work all stitches in M from here. *K2, K2tog* all stitches (9 sts)
**Row 25** Cast on 9 stitches at the beginning of the row, K9, Kfbf, Kfbf, K4, Kfbf, Kfbf, K1 (26 sts)
<u>**Row 26**</u> Cast on 9 stitches at the beginning of the row, P all stitches (35 sts)
**Row 27** Kfb, K to the last two stitches, Kfb, K1 (37 sts)
**Row 29** K
**Row 31** K1, SKP, K to the last three stitches, K2tog, K1 (35 sts)
**Row 33** Cast (bind) off 10 stitches, K to the end of the row (25 sts)
<u>**Row 34**</u> Cast (bind) off 10 stitches, P to the end of the row (15 sts)
**Rows 35–59** Work from the top piece pattern, including the right leg, tail and left leg.

### EARS – Make Four Pieces
Cast on 6 stitches in M.
**Row 2** P all even rows.
**Row 3** K
**Row 5** K1, SKP, K2tog, K1 (4 sts)
**Row 7** Cast (bind) off.

### SEWING UP
Weave in the loose ends. Take the top and under pieces and place the wrong sides together. Sew up using a mattress stitch in the corresponding coloured yarn, leaving a hole for stuffing. Only stuff the head and legs, leaving the body flat. Sew up the hole in the body. A top customer tip from the bear coasters in my previous book *Faux Taxidermy Knits* was to add dried lavender when stuffing.

Embroider the nose on the centre of the snout using the black DK yarn. Sew two diagonal lines on the snout, each measuring 1.5cm (½in), and add a vertical line in the centre below where they meet. This line should measure 0.5cm (¼in). Embroider a few dots using the black DK yarn either side of the snout.

Measure 3cm (1¼in) from the cast on edge and embroider two lines using black DK yarn that each measure 1cm (⅜in), leaving a gap of 1.5cm (½in) in the centre between them. Pull one of the lines down and add a small stitch in the centre to make a sleepy eye. Repeat for the second eye and weave in the loose ends. Take two ear pieces and place the wrong sides together. Sew up using a mattress stitch in M, leaving the cast on edges open. Add a small amount of stuffing. Repeat for the second ear. Place the ears 5cm (2in) from the cast on edge, leaving a gap of 3.5cm (1½in) in the centre between them. They will fit in the gaps where there are no loop stitches. Sew into place using M.

On the end of each leg embroider three lines using the black DK yarn; each line should measure 1.5cm (½in). Starting in the centre of the leg, embroider the first line vertically on the top piece of the knit. Then sew back into the first point and embroider the second line to the right of the first. Sew back into the first point and then embroider the third line to the left of the first. Weave in all the loose ends.

**1**. The loop stitch is very similar to Kfb. Start by knitting into the front of the stitch as per normal. Do not throw the worked stitch off the needle.

**2**. Take the yarn and pull it between the middle of the needles, over the stitch just knitted.

**3**. For the lion measure 3cm (1¼in) of the yarn pulled forwards, then take it back between the gap to create the loop. The size of loop may change for different patterns.

**4**. Once the yarn is back where it started, knit through the back of the stitch. Be careful not to pull the yarn too tightly or you'll lose your loop.

**5**. Transfer the stitch to the right-hand needle. The loop will be secure. You'll have made an additional stitch during this process. Place the left-hand needle into the second stitch on the right-hand needle.

**6**. Then pass the second stitch over the first. This is similar to casting (binding) off. Repeat this for every loop stitch needed.

# TRICERATOPS SLIPPERS

Get snuggly in these Triceratops Slippers. The merino wool makes them extra warm and adding some sock stop to the bottom stops them from slipping.

## MATERIALS
Yarn Stories Fine Merino DK, 100% fine merino, 120m per 50g (131yd per 1¾oz), or any DK yarn (merino wool naturally regulates temperature)
**M** - Leaf x 2 balls for S and M sizes or x 3 balls for L size
**C** - Spring Green x 1 ball for all sizes
4mm (US 6) straight needles, stitch holder, Rico Sock Stop - Yellow, a tiny amount of toy stuffing

## SHOE SIZES - WOMEN
**Small**
UK 2-4.5 | EU 35-37 | US 4-6
**Medium**
UK 5-7.5 | EU 37-39 | US 7-9
**Large**
UK 8-10 | EU 40-42 | US 10-12

## SHOE SIZES - MEN
**Large**
UK 6-11 | EU 39-46 | US 7-12

## TENSION (GAUGE)
22 sts x 30 rows = 10cm (4in)

## BEGINNER'S TIP
The rows from Row 7 on all sizes will look like this: **KX, *Kfb* three times, K4, *Kfb* three times, KX.** Read them like this: Knit the first number of stitches stated (X), then Kfb three times, then knit 4 stitches, then Kfb three times, then knit the number of stitches stated (X). Instructions between * and * are repeated; the number of times they are repeated is stated afterwards.

## SMALL SIZE SLIPPERS – Make Two
Cast on 54 stitches in M.
**Rows 2-6** *K1, P1* all stitches
**Row 7** K22, *Kfb* three times, K4, *Kfb* three times, K22 (60 sts)
**Row 8** P all even rows until otherwise stated.
**Row 9** K22, *Kfb, K1* three times, K4, *Kfb, K1* three times, K22 (66 sts)
**Row 11** K22, *Kfb, K2* three times, K4, *Kfb, K2* three times, K22 (72 sts)
**Row 13** K22, *Kfb, K3* three times, K4, *Kfb, K3* three times, K22 (78 sts)
**Row 15** K22, *Kfb, K4* three times, K4, *Kfb, K4* three times, K22 (84 sts)
**Row 17** K22, *Kfb, K5* three times, K4, *Kfb, K5* three times, K22 (90 sts)
**Row 19** K22, *Kfb, K6* three times, K4, *Kfb, K6* three times, K22 (96 sts)
**Row 21** K
**Row 23** K
**Row 25** K
**Row 27** K
**Row 29** K
**Row 31** K

**Row 33** Cast (bind) off 13 stitches, K to the end of the row (83 sts)
**Row 34** Cast (bind) off 13 stitches, P to the end of the row (70 sts)
**Row 35** Cast (bind) off 2 stitches, K to the end of the row (68 sts)
**Row 36** Cast (bind) off 2 stitches, P to the end of the row (66 sts)
**Row 37** Cast (bind) off 2 stitches, K to the end of the row (64 sts)
**Row 38** Cast (bind) off 2 stitches, P to the end of the row (62 sts)
**Row 39** Cast (bind) off 1 stitch, K to the end of the row (61 sts)
**Row 40** Cast (bind) off 1 stitch, P to the end of the row (60 sts)
**Row 41** Cast (bind) off 1 stitch, K to the end of the row (59 sts)
**Row 42** Cast (bind) off 1 stitch, P to the end of the row (58 sts)
**Row 43** Cast (bind) off all stitches.

## MEDIUM SIZE SLIPPERS – Make Two
Cast on 60 stitches in M.
**Rows 2-6** *K1, P1* all stitches
**Row 7** K25, *Kfb* three times, K4, *Kfb* three times, K25 (66 sts)
**Row 8** P all even rows until otherwise stated.
**Row 9** K25, *Kfb, K1* three times, K4, *Kfb, K1* three times, K25 (72 sts)
**Row 11** K25, *Kfb, K2* three times, K4, *Kfb, K2* three times, K25 (78 sts)
**Row 13** K25, *Kfb, K3* three times, K4, *Kfb, K3* three times, K25 (84 sts)

**Row 15** K25, *Kfb, K4* three times, K4, *Kfb, K4* three times, K25 (90 sts)

**Row 17** K25, *Kfb, K5* three times, K4, *Kfb, K5* three times, K25 (96 sts)

**Row 19** K25, *Kfb, K6* three times, K4, *Kfb, K6* three times, K25 (102 sts)

**Row 21** K25, *Kfb, K7* three times, K4, *Kfb, K7* three times, K25 (108 sts)

**Row 23** K25, *Kfb, K8* three times, K4, *Kfb, K8* three times, K25 (114 sts)

**Row 25** K

**Row 27** K

**Row 29** K

**Row 31** K

**Row 33** K

**Row 35** K

**Row 37** Cast (bind) off 16 stitches, K to the end of the row (98 sts)

**Row 38** Cast (bind) off 16 stitches, P to the end of the row (82 sts)

**Row 39** Cast (bind) off 4 stitches, K to the end of the row (78 sts)

**Row 40** Cast (bind) off 4 stitches, P to the end of the row (74 sts)

**Row 41** Cast (bind) off 3 stitches, K to the end of the row (71 sts)

**Row 42** Cast (bind) off 3 stitches, P to the end of the row (68 sts)

**Row 43** Cast (bind) off 2 stitches, K to the end of the row (66 sts)

**Row 44** Cast (bind) off 2 stitches, P to the end of the row (64 sts)

**Row 45** Cast (bind) off 2 stitches, K to the end of the row (62 sts)

**Row 46** Cast (bind) off 2 stitches, P to the end of the row (60 sts)

**Row 47** Cast (bind) off all stitches.

**LARGE SIZE SLIPPERS** – Make Two
Cast on 66 stitches in M.

**Rows 2-6** *K1, P1* all stitches

**Row 7** K28, *Kfb* three times, K4, *Kfb* three times, K28 (72 sts)

**Row 8** P all even rows until otherwise stated.

**Row 9** K28, *Kfb, K1* three times, K4, *Kfb, K1* three times, K28 (78 sts)

**Row 11** K28, *Kfb, K2* three times, K4, *Kfb, K2* three times, K28 (84 sts)

**Row 13** K28, *Kfb, K3* three times, K4, *Kfb, K3* three times, K28 (90 sts)

**Row 15** K28, *Kfb, K4* three times, K4, *Kfb, K4* three times, K28 (96 sts)

**Row 17** K28, *Kfb, K5* three times, K4, *Kfb, K5* three times, K28 (102 sts)

**Row 19** K28, *Kfb, K6* three times, K4, *Kfb, K6* three times, K28 (108 sts)

**Row 21** K28, *Kfb, K7* three times, K4, *Kfb, K7* three times, K28 (114 sts)

**Row 23** K28, *Kfb, K8* three times, K4, *Kfb, K8* three times, K28 (120 sts)

**Row 25** K

**Row 27** K

**Row 29** K

**Row 31** K

**Row 33** K

**Row 35** K

**Row 37** K

**Row 39** K

**Row 41** K

**Row 43** Cast (bind) off 16 stitches, K to the end of the row (104 sts)

**Row 44** Cast (bind) off 16 stitches, P to the end of the row (88 sts)

**Row 45** Cast (bind) off 4 stitches, K to the end of the row (84 sts)

**Row 46** Cast (bind) off 4 stitches, P to the end of the row (80 sts)

**Row 47** Cast (bind) off 3 stitches, K to the end of the row (77 sts)

**Row 48** Cast (bind) off 3 stitches, P to the end of the row (74 sts)

**Row 49** Cast (bind) off 2 stitches, K to the end of the row (72 sts)

**Row 50** Cast (bind) off 2 stitches, P to the end of the row (70 sts)

**Row 51** Cast (bind) off 2 stitches, K to the end of the row (68 sts)

**Row 52** Cast (bind) off 2 stitches, P to the end of the row (66 sts)

**Row 53** Cast (bind) off all stitches.

## FRILLS – Make Four Pieces

Cast on 24 stitches in M.

**Row 2** P all even rows until otherwise stated.

**Row 3** *Kfb, K3* all stitches (30 sts)

**Row 5** K

**Row 7** *Kfb, K4* all stitches (36 sts)

**Row 9** K

**Row 11** *Kfb, K5* all stitches (42 sts)

**Row 13** K

**Row 15** *Kfb, K6* all stitches (48 sts)

**Row 17** K

**Row 19** K

**Row 21** Change to C, working all stitches in it from here. K

*Spike One*

**Row 23** K6, TURN, placing the remaining 42 stitches on a holder to be worked later.

**Row 24** P the 6 stitches

**Row 25** K1, SKP, K2tog, K1 (4 sts)

**Row 26** P

**Row 27** Cast (bind) off.

*Spike Two*

Move 6 stitches from the holder onto the left-hand needle ready to be worked from Row 23.

**Row 23** Reattach the yarn and K the 6 stitches.

**Row 24** P

**Row 25** K1, SKP, K2tog, K1 (4 sts)

**Row 26** P

**Row 27** Cast (bind) off.

*Spikes Three–Eight*

Repeat the instructions for spike two. You will have eight spikes in total.

## SMALL HORNS – Make Two

Cast on 15 stitches in C.

**Row 2** P all even rows

**Row 3** K

**Row 5** *K3, K2tog* all stitches (12 sts)

**Row 7** *K2, K2tog* all stitches (9 sts)

**Row 9** *K1, K2tog* all stitches (6 sts)

**Row 11** *K2tog* all stitches (3 sts)

Cut the yarn leaving a tail. Thread it through the remaining three stitches and pull tightly. Then sew from the thread-through end to the cast on edge using a mattress stitch. Leave the cast on edges open.

## LONG HORNS – Make Four

Cast on 15 stitches in C.

**Row 2** P all even rows

**Row 3** K

**Row 5** K

**Row 7** *K3, K2tog* all stitches (12 sts)

**Row 9** K

**Row 11** *K2, K2tog* all stitches (9 sts)

**Row 13** *K1, K2tog* all stitches (6 sts)

**Row 15** *K2tog* all stitches (3 sts)

Cut the yarn leaving a tail. Thread it through the remaining three stitches and pull tightly. Then sew from the thread-through end to the cast on edge using a mattress stitch. Leave the cast on edges open.

## SEWING UP

Weave in the loose ends. Lay the slipper so the rib is facing down. Sew along the cast (bound) off edge, up the side of the back of the slipper to the cast on edge using a mattress stitch in M. Add some sock stop to the base of the slipper, along the cast (bound) off edge. If you haven't used sock stop before, practise on a scrap of fabric first. We'd recommend going up to 2cm (¾in) either side of the cast (bound) off edge. You can decorate your slipper in any way you'd like. Repeat for the second slipper. Leave to dry for 6–8 hours.

Lay the slipper so the cast (bound) off edge is flat against a table and the top of the slipper is facing you. For all sizes: take the small horn and stuff. Then place it 2cm (¾in) from the point of the front of the slipper. Sew into place using C.

Take two frill pieces and place the wrong sides together. Sew up using a mattress stitch in the corresponding coloured yarn, leaving the cast on edges open. Add a small amount of stuffing to the frill, keeping it flat. Repeat for the second frill. On all sizes: sew the frill across the slipper, just before the ribbed part. Sew the cast on edges of the frill against the slipper using M. Leave the edge slightly open so the frill will stand up straight. Take two long horns and add a small amount of stuffing. Place them 1cm (⅜in) down from the frill towards the point of the slipper, leaving a gap of 2cm (¾in) in the centre between them. Sew into place using C.

Embroider the eyes using C. Measure 1.5cm (½in) directly below one of the large horns and sew a small line measuring 1cm (⅜in) . Then push the line down and add a small stitch in the centre to make a sleepy eye. Repeat for the second eye, leaving a gap of 2cm (¾in) in the centre between them. Repeat for the second slipper. Weave in the loose ends.

# CRAFTY CROSSWORD

**DOWN**

**1** Mysterious circuit (5,4)
**2** The knitting social network (7)
**3** Vintage knitting pins that won't slow you down (13)
**6** A Dutch brand that translates to 'Little Ships' (9)
**9** A sweet variegated wool (4,4)

**ACROSS**

**3** A technique that combines the best of knitting and crochet (8)
**4** Corded knitting from the Continent (6)
**5** *K1, P1* all stitches (3,6)
**6** Pass the _____ stitch over (7)
**7** Wool from a goat (8)
**8** UK slang name for a place known for its ice rink, fireworks and knitting shows (4,5)

# The Knitter's Alphabet

The comprehensive-ish A to Z guide to knitting.

## Aa
### is for Aran

Named after the Aran Islands, these complex knits take ages but look fabulous.

## Bb
### is for Blocking

Spray it or submerge it, pin it, reshape it and see those stitches transform.

# Cc
## is for Crochet

It's cool but it's not quite knitting.

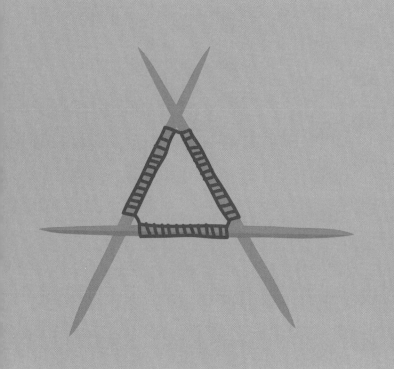

# Dd
## is for DPNs

Love them or hate them, just make sure your stitches don't fall off them.

# Ee
## is for Embroidery

Can't do intarsia? Try embroidery for nearly the same effect.

# Ff
## is for Frogged

When you undo your work and it sounds like a frog, 'rip it, rip it'.

Rip it
Rip it

# Gg
## is for Garter

Knit every row. Great for scarves, blankets and beginners.

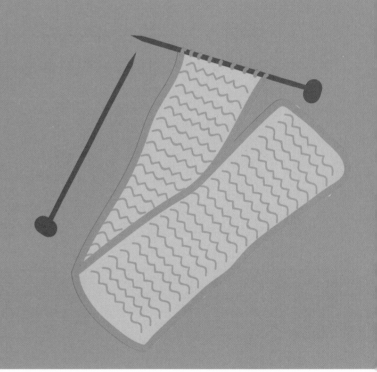

# Hh
## is for Hand Wash

Things will last longer when you look after them. Hand wash your knits – they're special.

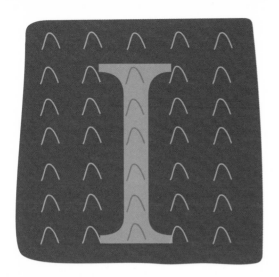

# Ii
## is for Intarsia

Multicoloured design that looks great, but often results in a tangle.

# Jj
## is for Jumper

Knit yourself a lovely jumper to keep warm.

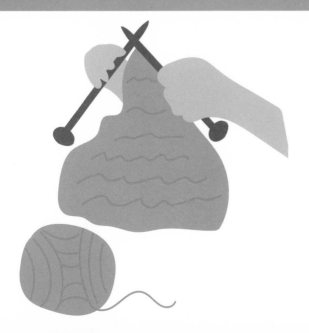

# Kk
## is for Knit

The most important letter in the alphabet. Never stop knitting.

# Ll
## is for LYS

Support your Local Yarn Shop; they've got good stuff there (mainly yarn).

# Mm
## is for MKAL

What could it be? It's a Mystery Knit Along. Watch this space.

# Nn
## is for Needles

Two powerful sticks that can make anything. Just add yarn.

# Oo

## is for Openwork

Holes, lace, whatever you want
to call it, it sure is pretty.

# Pp
## is for Purl

Nobody really likes purling,
but it's something you have to do.

# Qq

## is for Queued

The endless list of projects you'd like
to do but haven't quite got round to yet.

# Rr
## is for in the Round

Working a pattern on DPNs or circular needles. Make sure you add a marker or you might lose your place.

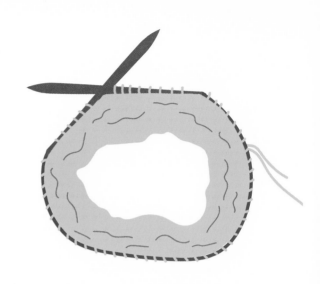

# Ss
## is for Stash

All the yarn you own, yes even that secret lot you've got in hiding.

# Tt
## is for Tension

The difference between a hat and a basket to keep your yarn in. (Also known as gauge.)

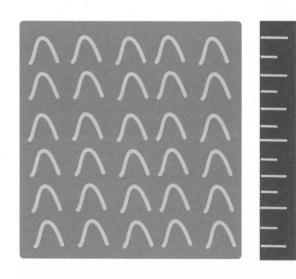

# Uu
## is for UFO

Finding a project and not being able to remember what it is, making it an unrecognizable object.

# Vv
## is for Vanilla

An easy, plain pattern; you know the type.

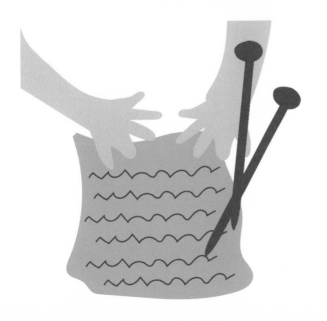

# Ww
## is for WIP

Your current work in progress; you've probably got ten of them.

# Xx
## is for X-ray

It's always worrying when your luggage containing your WIP goes through the X-ray.

# Yy
## is for Yarn

It comes in all types of shapes, weights, sizes and colours. Give it a squish.

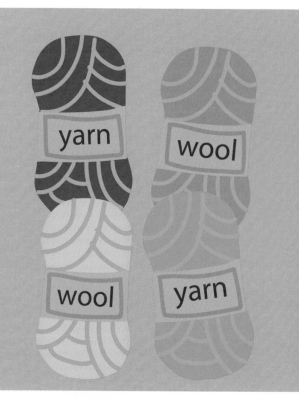

# Zz
## is for Zigzag

Create a pretty chevron scarf using a zigzag pattern.

# SHOULD I KNIT TODAY?

Do you ask yourself this daily? Well, here's the answer!

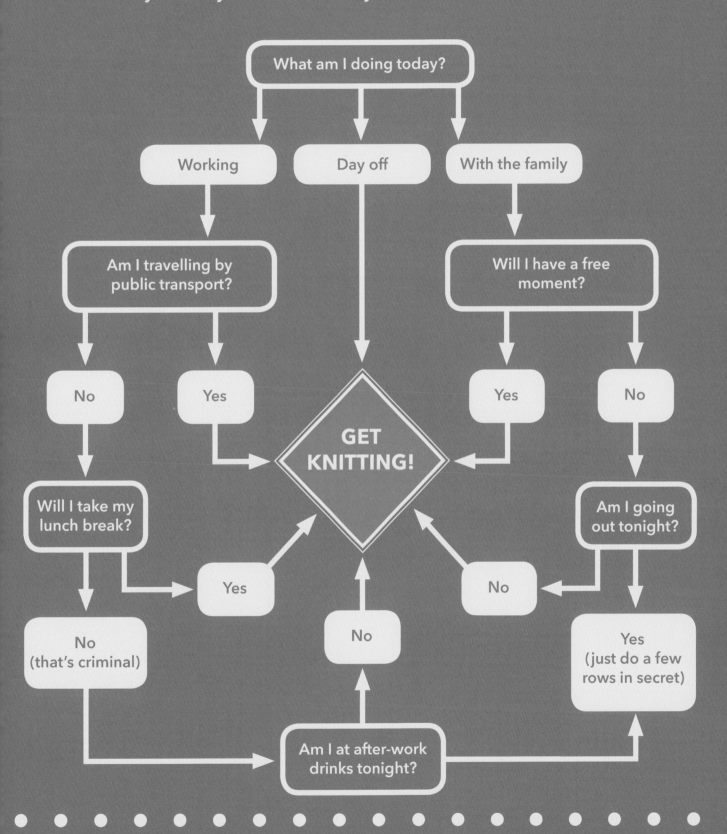

CATCH OF THE DAY

lobster dinner

# LOBSTER DINNER – SERVES ONE
## MATERIALS

Sincerely Louise How Does It Feel, 100% wool, 115m per 100g
(126yd per 3½oz), or any lightweight chunky (bulky) yarn
**M** – Red – Encouraged x 2 balls
6mm (US 10) straight needles, stitch holder,
2 x 10mm toy eyes and washers, 50g (1¾oz) toy stuffing
**Tension (Gauge):** 16 sts x 20 rows = 10cm (4in)
**Finished Size:** 46 x 34 x 8cm (18 x 13½ x 3¼in)

**TOP PIECE – Make One**
Cast on 6 stitches in M.
**Row 2** P all even rows unless
  otherwise stated. Even rows
  have been <u>underlined</u>.
**Row 3** *Kfb* all stitches
  (12 sts)
**Row 5** K
**Row 7** K
**Row 9** *Kfb, K3* all stitches
  (15 sts)
**Row 11** K
**Row 13** K
**Row 15** K
<u>**Row 16**</u> K
**Row 17** K
**Row 19** K
**Row 21** K
**Row 23** K
**Row 25** K1, SKP, K to the last
  three stitches, K2tog, K1
  (13 sts)
<u>**Row 26**</u> K
**Row 27** Kfb, K to the last two
  stitches, Kfb, K1 (15 sts)
**Row 29** K
<u>**Row 30**</u> K
**Row 31** K
**Row 33** K
**Row 35** K
<u>**Row 36**</u> K
**Row 37** K
**Row 39** K1, SKP, K to the last

three stitches, K2tog, K1
  (13 sts)
**Row 41** K
<u>**Row 42**</u> K
**Row 43** K
**Row 45** K1, SKP, K to the last
  three stitches, K2tog, K1
  (11 sts)
**Row 47** K
<u>**Row 48**</u> K
**Row 49** K
**Row 51** K1, SKP, K to the last
  three stitches, K2tog, K1
  (9 sts)
**Row 53** K
<u>**Row 54**</u> K
**Row 55** K
**Row 57** *Kfb, K2* all stitches
  (12 sts)
**Row 59** *Kfb, K1* all stitches
  (18 sts)
**Row 61** K
**Row 63** K
**Row 65** K
**Row 67** Cast (bind) off.

**UNDER PIECE – Make One**
Cast on 6 stitches in M.
**Row 2** P all even rows.
**Row 3** *Kfb* all stitches
  (12 sts)
**Row 5** K
**Row 7** K

**Row 9** *Kfb, K3* all stitches
  (15 sts)
**Rows 11-24** Work in St st
**Row 25** K1, SKP, K to the last
  three stitches, K2tog, K1
  (13 sts)
**Row 27** Kfb, K to the last two
  stitches, Kfb, K1 (15 sts)
**Rows 29-38** Work in St st
**Row 39** K1, SKP, K to the last
  three stitches, K2tog, K1
  (13 sts)
**Row 41** K
**Row 43** K
**Row 45** K1, SKP, K to the last
  three stitches, K2tog, K1
  (11 sts)
**Row 47** K
**Row 49** K
**Row 51** K1, SKP, K to the last
  three stitches, K2tog, K1
  (9 sts)
**Row 53** K
**Row 55** K
**Row 57** *Kfb, K2* all stitches
  (12 sts)
**Row 59** *Kfb, K1* all stitches
  (18 sts)
**Row 61** K
**Row 63** K
**Row 65** K
**Row 67** Cast (bind) off.

SEE OUR DAILY SPECIALS BOARD

## CLAWS - Side One - Make Two
Cast on 8 stitches in M.
**Row 2** P all even rows.
**Row 3** K
**Row 5** K
**Row 7** K
**Row 9** Kfb, Kfbf, K2tog, K2tog, K2tog (8 sts)
**Row 11** Kfb, Kfbf, K2tog, K2tog, K2tog (8 sts)
**Row 13** Kfb, Kfbf, K2tog, K2tog, K2tog (8 sts)
**Row 15** Kfb, Kfbf, K2tog, K2tog, K2tog (8 sts)
**Row 17** Kfb, Kfbf, K2tog, K2tog, K2tog (8 sts)
**Row 19** Kfb, K to the last two stitches, Kfb, K1 (10 sts)
**Row 21** K
**Row 23** Kfb, K to the last two stitches, Kfb, K1 (12 sts)
**Row 25** K

### Right Side of Claw One
**Row 27** Kfb, K2, Kfb, K1 (7 sts), TURN, placing the remaining 7 stitches on a holder to be worked later.
**Row 29** K
**Row 31** K1, SKP, K4 (6 sts)
**Row 33** K1, SKP, K3 (5 sts)
**Row 35** K1, SKP, K2 (4 sts)
**Row 37** K1, SKP, K1 (3 sts)
**Row 39** Cast (bind) off.

### Left Side of Claw One
Move the 7 stitches from the holder onto the left-hand needle ready to be worked from Row 27.
**Row 27** Reattach the yarn and K1, Kfb, K3, Kfb, K1 (9 sts)
**Row 29** K
**Row 31** K6, K2tog, K1 (8 sts)
**Row 33** K5, K2tog, K1 (7 sts)

**Row 35** K2, K2tog, K2tog, K1 (5 sts)
**Row 37** K2tog, K2tog, K1 (3 sts)
**Row 39** Cast (bind) off.

## CLAWS - Side Two - Make Two
Cast on 8 stitches in M.
**Row 2** P all even rows.
**Row 3** K
**Row 5** K
**Row 7** K
**Row 9** SKP, SKP, SKP, Kfbf, Kfb (8 sts)
**Row 11** SKP, SKP, SKP, Kfbf, Kfb (8 sts)
**Row 13** SKP, SKP, SKP, Kfbf, Kfb (8 sts)
**Row 15** SKP, SKP, SKP, Kfbf, Kfb (8 sts)
**Row 17** SKP, SKP, SKP, Kfbf, Kfb (8 sts)
**Row 19** Kfb, K to the last two stitches, Kfb, K1 (10 sts)
**Row 21** K
**Row 23** Kfb, K to the last two stitches, Kfb, K1 (12 sts)
**Row 25** K

### Right Side of Claw Two
**Row 27** Kfb, K4, Kfb, K1 (9 sts), TURN, placing the remaining 5 stitches on a holder to be worked later.
**Row 29** K
**Row 31** K1, SKP, K6 (8 sts)
**Row 33** K1, SKP, K5 (7 sts)
**Row 35** K1, SKP, SKP, K2 (5 sts)
**Row 37** K1, SKP, SKP (3 sts)
**Row 39** Cast (bind) off

### Left Side of Claw Two
Move the 5 stitches from the holder onto the left-hand needle ready to be worked from Row 27.
**Row 27** Reattach the yarn

and K1, Kfb, K1, Kfb, K1 (7 sts)
**Row 29** K
**Row 31** K4, K2tog, K1 (6 sts)
**Row 33** K3, K2tog, K1 (5 sts)
**Row 35** K2, K2tog, K1 (4 sts)
**Row 37** K1, K2tog, K1 (3 sts)
**Row 39** Cast (bind) off.

## BIG LEGS - Make Four
Cast on 7 stitches in M.
**Row 2** P
**Rows 3-26** Work in St st
**Row 27** K1, K2tog, K2tog, K2tog (4 sts)
**Row 28** P
**Row 29** Cast (bind) off and sew up from the cast (bound) off edge to the cast on edge using a mattress stitch.

## SMALL LEGS - Make Four
Cast on 7 stitches in M.
**Row 2** P
**Rows 3-20** Work in St st
**Row 21** K1, K2tog, K2tog, K2tog (4 sts)
**Row 22** P
**Row 23** Cast (bind) off and sew up from the cast (bound) off edge to the cast on edge using a mattress stitch.

## ANTENNAS - Make Two
Cast on 5 stitches in M.
**Row 2** P
**Rows 3-32** Work in St st
**Row 33** K1, K2tog, K2tog (3 sts)
**Row 34** P
**Row 35** Cast (bind) off and sew up from the cast (bound) off edge to the cast on edge using a mattress stitch.
Weave in all loose ends.

# SEWING UP

### The Body
Take the top and under pieces and place the wrong sides together. Sew up using a mattress stitch in M, leaving a hole for stuffing. Stuff the lobster following the shape of the knit. Do not sew up the hole yet.

### The Face
Place the eyes on the face 3.5cm (1½in) from the cast on edge, leaving a gap of 4cm (1½in) in the centre between them. Secure into place using washers, then sew up the hole in the body. Sew the two antenna pieces onto the centre front of the lobster, along the cast on edge seam, leaving a gap of 0.5cm (¼in) between them.

### The Claws
Take a side one and side two claw piece and place the wrong sides together. Sew up using a mattress stitch in M, leaving the cast on edges open. Repeat for the second claw. Add a small amount of stuffing to the base of the claws. Place the first claw 4cm (1½in) from the cast on edge, along the right side of the body. The first line on the lobster's body should be in the centre of the claw's cast on edge. Sew into place using M and repeat for the second claw, placing it on the left-hand side of the body.

### The Legs
Place one of the big legs 1cm (⅜in) down from the claw on the right-hand side of the body. Sew into place using M. Sew the next big leg 1cm (⅜in) down from the first one placed. Then sew a small leg 0.5cm (¼in) from the big leg just placed. Finally sew a small leg 1cm (⅜in) from the small leg previously placed. Mirror these instructions for the legs on the left-hand side of the lobster. Weave in the loose ends.

## SHEFFIELD, UK

*Contains wool; please inform your waiter of any allergies.

# FIND THE FIBRE

```
C L N J L T C H C S Y H O Y W
K A N Y Q O N C I X I M D K G
R A S I L G B L K I M L E W Z
I L P H R O P U I V B S K A W
A I G I M S N L Q O I J Z P Y
H N C D B E M W T A C A P L A
O E Q W B N R T A O B R E R M
M N P L D R O E O B A N A N A
A T Z T A M J B A O T K W E N
C N J H T N M N V I K M L F R
R X F B Z A O Q O N I R E M I
Y M T A B A W T T A P D L V A
L V T T S J N Q T L C S J D H
I H O A O C J F P O Q Z M H O
C R L O O W A J K Q C C Z S M
```

**ACRYLIC**        **ALPACA**        **BAMBOO**

**BANANA**        **CASHMERE**        **COTTON**

**LINEN**        **MERINO**        **MOHAIR**

**NYLON**        **SILK**        **WOOL**

# FAUX FARM TAXIDERMY
## ANIMAL-FRIENDLY KNITS

# FAUX TAXIDERMY MINI HEADS

### MATERIALS
Rico Essentials Acrylic Antipilling DK, 100% acrylic, 250m per 100g (273yd per 3½oz),
or any DK yarn (antipilling yarn makes a smooth texture and nice sheen)
x 1 ball of each colour plus small amount of black DK yarn for embroidery if not making the cow

### TENSION (GAUGE)
21 sts x 28 rows = 10cm (4in) on 4mm (US 6) knitting needles

### SCRAP YARN MARKERS
Colour X – Eye placement    Colour Y – Ear placement    Colour Z – Horn placement

| DONKEY | PIG | COW |
|---|---|---|
| **M** – Grey | **M** – Pink | **M** – Pink |
| **C** – Cream | **C** – Cream | **B** – Black |
| 20g (¾oz) toy stuffing | 20g (¾oz) toy stuffing | **C** – Cream |
| 2 x 10mm toy eyes and washers | 2 x 10mm toy eyes and washers | 20g (¾oz) toy stuffing |
| Mini backing board (see page 35) | Mini backing board (see page 35) | 2 x 10mm toy eyes and washers |
|  |  | Mini backing board (see page 35) |

**FINISHED SIZE**
13 x 15 x 11cm (5 x 6 x 4¼in)

**FINISHED SIZE**
13 x 14 x 12cm (5 x 5½ x 4¾in)

**FINISHED SIZE**
16 x 14 x 14cm (6¼ x 5½ x 5½in)

**TOP PIECE – Make One**
Cast on 5 stitches in C.
**Row 2** P all even rows unless otherwise stated. P rows have been underlined.
**Row 3** *Kfb* all stitches (10 sts)
**Row 5** K
**Row 7** Cast (bind) off.
Pick up the 10 cast (bound) off stitches using M; this will become Row 9. (*Tip: by casting (binding) off and then picking up the stitches, the knit creates a flatter snout for the pig.*)
**Row 10** P
**Row 11** Kfb, K7, Kfb, K1 (12 sts)
**Row 13** K
**Row 15** *Kfb, K1* all stitches (18 sts)
**Row 17** *Kfb, K2* all stitches (24 sts)
**Row 18** P [add colour X scrap yarn markers to the 8th and 18th stitches]
**Row 19** *Kfb, K3* all stitches (30 sts)
**Rows 21-26** Work in St st
**Row 27** K [add colour Y scrap yarn markers to the 4th, 12th, 18th and 26th stitches]
**Row 29** K
**Row 31** K
**Row 33** *K3, K2tog* all stitches (24 sts)
**Row 35** K
**Row 37** *K2, K2tog* all stitches (18 sts)
**Row 39** K
**Row 41** *K1, K2tog* all stitches (12 sts)
**Row 43** K
**Row 45** Cast (bind) off loosely.

**UNDER PIECE – Make One**
Cast on 5 stitches in C.
**Row 2** P all even rows unless otherwise stated. P rows have been underlined.
**Row 3** *Kfb* all stitches (10 sts)
**Row 5** K
**Row 7** Cast (bind) off.
Pick up the 10 cast (bound) off stitches using M; this will become Row 9.
**Row 10** P
**Row 11** Kfb, K7, Kfb, K1 (12 sts)
**Row 13** K
**Row 15** *Kfb, K1* all stitches (18 sts)
**Row 17** K
**Row 19** *Kfb, K2* all stitches (24 sts)

**Rows 21-26** Work in St st
**Row 27** *K2, K2tog* all stitches (18 sts)
**Row 29** *Kfb, K2* all stitches (24 sts)
**Row 31** *Kfb, K3* all stitches (30 sts)
**Row 33** K
**Row 35** *Kfb, K4* all stitches (36 sts)
**Row 37** K
**Row 39** *Kfb, K5* all stitches (42 sts)
**Row 41** K
**Row 43** *Kfb, K6* all stitches (48 sts)
**Row 45** Cast (bind) off loosely.

**RIGHT EAR – Make One**
Cast on 9 stitches in M.
**Rows 2-8** Knit every row.
**Row 9** K1, SKP, SKP, K4 (7 sts)
**Row 10** K all even rows from here.
**Row 11** K1, SKP, K4 (6 sts)
**Row 13** K
**Row 15** K1, SKP, K2tog, K1 (4 sts)
**Row 17** Cast (bind) off.

**LEFT EAR – Make One**
Cast on 9 stitches in M.
**Rows 2-8** Knit every row.
**Row 9** K4, K2tog, K2tog, K1 (7 sts)
**Row 10** K all even rows from here.
**Row 11** K4, K2tog, K1 (6 sts)
**Row 13** K
**Row 15** K1, SKP, K2tog, K1 (4 sts)
**Row 17** Cast (bind) off.

**SEWING UP**
*Head: Follow these instructions for all of the mini heads.* Weave in all the loose ends. Take the top and under pieces and place the wrong sides together. Sew up from the cast (bound) off edge to the cast on edge using a mattress stitch in M. Then sew along the other side of the head, from the cast on edge to the cast (bound) off edge. Leave the cast (bound) off edges

open. Stuff the head following the shape of the knit, being careful not to overstuff.
*Eyes: Follow these instructions for all of the mini heads.* Place the 10mm eyes over the colour X scrap yarn markers. Remove the markers and secure the eyes using the washers.
*Nostrils:* Embroider two nostrils using the black DK yarn on the centre of the seam of the snout. Each line should measure 1cm (⅜in) with a gap of 0.5cm (¼in) between them.
*Ears:* Place the right ear between the right-hand set of colour Y scrap yarn markers. To make the ear stand up, sew the first row on the front of the ear against the knit of the head. Then sew the second row on the back of the ear against the knit of the head. Repeat for the left ear, placing it between the left-hand set of colour Y scrap yarn markers and sewing it into place using M. Remove all markers and weave in the loose ends.

# COW

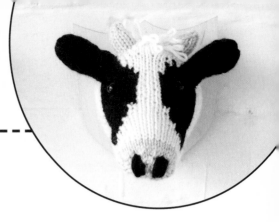

## TOP PIECE – Make One

Cast on 5 stitches in M.
**Row 2** P all even rows until stated.
**Row 3** *Kfb* all stitches (10 sts)
**Row 5** *Kfb, K1* all stitches (15 sts)
**Row 7** K
**Row 9** Cast (bind) off.
Pick up the 15 cast (bound) off stitches using C; this will become Row 11 (see tip on pig pattern).
**Row 12** P
**Row 13** K
**Row 14** P
**Row 15** K2B, K11C, K2B
**Row 16** P3B, P9C, P3B
**Row 17** K4B, K7C, K4B
**Row 18** P4B, P7C, P4B
**Row 19** K5B, K5C, K5B
**Row 20** P5B, P5C, P5B
**Rows 21–22** Repeat Rows 19–20.
**Row 23** Kfb in B, K5B, K3C, K4B, Kfb in B, K1B (17 sts)
**Row 24** P7B, P3C, P7B
**Row 25** K1B, Kfb in B, K5B, K3C, K4B, Kfb in B, K2B (19 sts)
**Row 26** P8B, P3C, P8B
**Row 27** K2B, Kfb in B, K5B, K3C, K4B, Kfb in B, K3B (21 sts)
**Row 28** P9B, P3C, P9B
**Row 29** K3B, Kfb in B, K5B, K3C, K4B, Kfb in B, K4B (23 sts)
**Row 30** P10B, P3C, P10B
**Row 31** K4B, Kfb in B, K5B, K3C, K4B, Kfb in B, K5B (25 sts)
**Row 32** P11B, P3C, P11B
**Row 33** K11B, K3C, K11B
**Row 34** P11B [add a colour X scrap yarn marker to the 7th of these 11 sts], P3C, P11B [add a colour X scrap yarn marker to the 5th of these 11 sts]
**Row 35** K10B, K5C, K10B
**Row 36** P10B, P5C, P10B
**Rows 37–38** Repeat Rows 35–36.
**Row 39** K9B, K7C, K9B
**Row 40** P9B, P7C, P9B
**Row 41** K8B, K9C, K8B
**Row 42** P8B, P9C, P8B
**Row 43** K8B, Kfb in C, K2C, Kfb in C, K2C, Kfb in C, K2C, K8B (28 sts)
**Row 44** P8B [add colour Y scrap yarn markers to the 1st and 8th of these eight sts], P12C, P8B [add colour Y scrap yarn markers to the 1st and 8th of these eight sts]
**Row 45** K6B, SKP in B, Kfb in C, K3C, Kfb in C, K3C, Kfb in C, K3C, K2tog in B, K6B (29 sts)
**Row 46** P6B, P17C, P6B
**Row 47** K5B, K7C, L1C, K1C, K1C, L1C, K7C, K5B
*Tip: L = loop stitch; see page 11. Each loop should measure 2cm (¾in).*
**Row 48** P5B, P19C, P5B
**Row 49** K4B, K1C, SKP in C, K4C, L1C, K1C, L1C, K1C, L1C, K1C, L1C, K4C, K2tog in C, K1C, K4B (27 sts)
**Row 50** P3B, P21C [add colour Z scrap yarn markers to the 1st, 5th, 17th and 21st of these 21 sts], P3B
**Row 51** K2B, K3C, SKP in C, K4C, L1C, K1C, L1C, K1C, L1C, K4C, K2tog in C, K3C, K2B (25 sts)
**Row 52** P2B, P21C, P2B
**Row 53** Work all stitches in C from here. *K3, K2tog* all stitches (20 sts)
**Row 54** P all even rows from here.
**Row 55** *K2, K2tog* all stitches (15 sts)
**Row 57** *K1, K2tog* all stitches (10 sts)
**Row 59** K
**Row 61** Cast (bind) off loosely.

## UNDER PIECE – Make One

Cast on 5 stitches in M.
**Row 2** P all even rows until stated.
**Rows 3–12** Repeat Rows 3–12 of the cow's under piece.
**Rows 13–32** Work in St st
**Row 33** *Kfb, K4* all stitches (18 sts)
**Row 35** K
**Row 37** *Kfb, K2* all stitches (24 sts)
**Row 39** K
**Row 41** *Kfb, K3* all stitches (30 sts)
**Row 43** K
**Row 45** *Kfb, K4* all stitches (36 sts)
**Row 47** *Kfb, K5* all stitches (42 sts)
**Row 49** *Kfb, K6* all stitches (48 sts)
**Rows 51–60** Work in St st
**Row 61** Cast (bind) off loosely.

## EARS – Make Four Pieces

Cast on 8 stitches in B.
**Row 2** P all even rows.
**Rows 3–6** Work in St st
**Row 7** K1, Kfb, K3, Kfb, K2 (10 sts)
**Rows 9–12** Work in St st
**Row 13** K1, SKP, K4, K2tog, K1 (8 sts)
**Row 15** K1, SKP, K2, K2tog, K1 (6 sts)
**Row 17** K1, SKP, K2tog, K1 (4 sts)
**Row 19** Cast (bind) off.

## HORNS – Make Two

Cast on 12 stitches in M.
**Row 2** P all even rows.
**Rows 3–6** Work in St st
**Row 7** *K1, K2tog* all stitches (8 sts)
**Row 9** *K2tog* all stitches (4 sts)
Cut the yarn leaving a tail for sewing up. Thread it through the remaining four stitches and pull tightly.

## SEWING UP

*Head and Eyes:* Follow the instructions for the pig, but use C for the mattress stitch.
*Nostrils:* Embroider two nostrils in the centre of the snout, each measuring 1.5cm (½in). Leave a gap of 0.5cm (¼in) in the centre between them.
*Ears:* Take a front and back ear piece and place the wrong sides together. Sew up using a mattress stitch in B, leaving the cast on edges open. Do not stuff. Repeat for the second ear. Place an ear between the right-hand set of colour Y scrap yarn markers. Sew onto the head using B. Repeat for the second ear, sewing it between the left-hand set of colour Y markers.
*Horns:* Add a tiny amount of stuffing to the horns. Place the first one between the right-hand set of colour Z scrap yarn markers. Sew the cast on edge of the horn against the knit of the head using M. Repeat for the second horn, sewing it between the left-hand set of colour Z markers. Remove all markers and weave in the loose ends.

# DONKEY

## TOP PIECE – Make One
Cast on 3 stitches in C.
**Row 2** P all even rows.
**Row 3** *Kfb* all stitches (6 sts)
**Row 5** *Kfb, K1* all stitches (9 sts)
**Row 7** *Kfb, K2* all stitches (12 sts)
**Rows 9–12** Work in St st
**Row 13** Change to M, working all stitches in it from here. K
**Row 15** Kfb, K2, Kfb, K3, Kfb, K2, Kfb, K1 (16 sts)
**Row 17** K1, Kfb, K to the last three stitches, Kfb, K2 (18 sts)
**Row 19** K2, Kfb, K3, Kfb, K3, Kfb, K3, Kfb, K3 (22 sts)
**Row 21** K3, Kfb, K13 [add a colour X scrap yarn marker to the 4th and 11th of these thirteen stitches], Kfb, K4 (24 sts)
**Row 23** K4, Kfb, K4, Kfb, K3, Kfb, K4, Kfb, K5 (28 sts)
**Row 25** K5, Kfb, K to the last seven stitches, Kfb, K6 (30 sts)
**Row 27** K12, Kfb, K1, Kfb, K1, Kfb, K13 (33 sts)
**Row 29** K6, SKP, K4, Kfb, K2, Kfb, K2, Kfb, K6, K2tog, K6 (34 sts)
**Row 31** K6, SKP, K18 [add colour Y scrap yarn markers to the 1st, 7th, 12th and 18th of these eighteen stitches], K2tog, K6 (32 sts)
**Row 33** K6, SKP, K16, K2tog, K6 (30 sts)
**Rows 35–42** Work in St st
**Row 43** *K3, K2tog* all stitches (24 sts)
**Row 45** *K2, K2tog* all stitches (18 sts)
**Row 47** *K1, K2tog* all stitches (12 sts)
**Row 49** K
**Row 51** Cast (bind) off loosely.

## UNDER PIECE – Make One
Cast on 3 stitches in C.
**Row 2** P all even rows.
**Row 3** *Kfb* all stitches (6 sts)
**Row 5** *Kfb, K1* all stitches (9 sts)
**Row 7** *Kfb, K2* all stitches (12 sts)
**Rows 9–12** Work in St st
**Row 13** Change to M, working all stitches in it from here. K
**Rows 15–24** Work in St st
**Row 25** *K2, K2tog* all stitches (9 sts)
**Row 27** *Kfb, K2* all stitches (12 sts)
**Row 29** K

**Row 31** *Kfb, K1* all stitches (18 sts)
**Row 33** K
**Row 35** *Kfb, K2* all stitches (24 sts)
**Row 37** K
**Row 39** *Kfb, K3* all stitches (30 sts)
**Row 41** K
**Row 43** *Kfb, K4* all stitches (36 sts)
**Row 45** K
**Row 47** *Kfb, K5* all stitches (42 sts)
**Row 49** *Kfb, K6* all stitches (48 sts)
**Row 51** Cast (bind) off loosely.

## EARS – Front Piece – Make Two
Cast on 6 stitches in M.
**Row 2** P
**Row 3** K2M, K2C, K2M
**Row 4** P2M, P2C, P2M
**Row 5** K2M, Kfb in C, Kfb in C, K2M (8 sts)
**Row 6** P2M, P4C, P2M
**Row 7** K2M, K4C, K2M
**Row 8** P2M, P4C, P2M
**Rows 9–12** Repeat Rows 7–8 twice more.
**Row 13** K1M, SKP in M, K2C, K2tog in M, K1M (6 sts)
**Row 14** P2M, P2C, P2M
**Row 15** K all stitches in M
**Row 16** P all stitches in M
**Row 17** Cast (bind) off in M.

## EARS – Back Piece – Make Two
Cast on 6 stitches in M.
**Row 2** P all even rows.
**Row 3** K
**Row 5** K2, Kfb, Kfb, K2 (8 sts)
**Rows 7–12** Work in St st
**Row 13** K1, SKP, K2, K2tog, K1 (6 sts)
**Row 15** K
**Row 17** Cast (bind) off.

## SEWING UP
**Head and Eyes:**
Follow the instructions for the pig.
**Nostrils:** Embroider two nostrils using the black DK yarn on the donkey's snout. Measure

1cm (⅜in) from the cast on edge seam and leave a gap of 1cm (⅜in) in the centre between them. Each nostril should measure 1.5cm (½in) and be at a slight diagonal angle, facing away from each other.
**Ears:** Take a front ear and back ear piece and place the wrong sides together. Sew up using a mattress stitch in M, leaving the cast on edges open. Add a small amount of stuffing. Repeat for the second ear. Place an ear between the right-hand set of colour Y scrap yarn markers. Sew the cast on edge of the ear against the knit of the head using M. Repeat for the second ear, placing it between the left-hand set of colour Y scrap yarn markers and sewing into place. Remove the markers and weave in the loose ends.
**Mane:** Use black DK yarn to embroider small loops on the top of the donkey's head; each loop should measure 2cm (¾in). Start in the centre of the two ears and, using that as a guide, embroider down to the cast (bound) off edge; this will create the donkey's mane. Weave in the loose ends.

# MOUNTING

**1.** Each animal head fits perfectly onto the Sincerely Louise mini backing board (see page 112). The back of the board is the side where the laser marks are. Using the yarn colour of the cast (bound) off row of the head, tie a small loop in the centre top hole and knot the yarn.

**2.** Place the head against the right side of the board (the side where there are no laser marks). The cast (bound) off edge of the knit should sit against the ring of holes. This example is shown on the cow; apply this technique to all of the heads.

**3.** Start by pulling the sewing up yarn through the centre top hole and into the cast (bound) off edge of the head.

**4.** Sew back into the head, a couple of stitches across from where the sewing needle was just pushed through. Push the needle and yarn through the hole next to the first one.

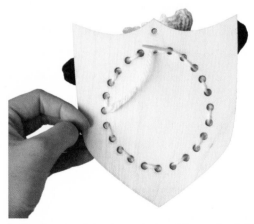

**5.** Sew into the next hole on the back of the board and then back into the head. Continue in this way around all the holes to create a running stitch.

**6.** The back of the board should now look like this. Repeat this stitching technique several times to secure the head. Add a small loop to the centre top hole for hanging.

# AT THE CRAFT FAIR

We love exhibiting at craft fairs. Our favourites in the UK are Unravel and Yarndale!

competition

1. How many balls of wool are there?

2. How many people are knitting?

3. Who's won first prize?

4. What shoes is Louise wearing?

5. How many animals are at the fair?

**Answers on page 110**  The Knitter's Activity Book

# Tension (Gauge)
## Why is it important?

**You wouldn't bake using the wrong temperature, so why knit in the wrong tension?**

Jenny once knitted a hat without checking her tension. When she finished, she found it was the size of a small basket. She laughed but you could tell she was disappointed. Before you start knitting, you're often asked to knit a tension square – a certain number of stitches and rows using a particular size needle. If your square is the right size then you're all good to cast on. If not, then your tension is incorrect. This means you have to adjust your needle size and try again. Getting the wrong tension will mean your project may not turn out as you hoped. Don't be a Jenny.

## Baking

*Ingredients*

*Temperature*

## Knitting

*Materials*

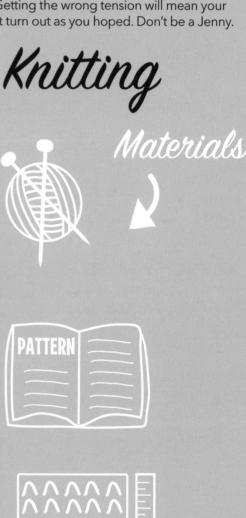

*Tension*

# LOLA THE POLAR BEAR MOVES HOME

Knit along with Lola as she travels across the globe and meets a host of adorable characters. Patterns from page 58.

# POLAR BEAR

**MATERIALS**
Sincerely Louise How Does It Feel, 100% wool, 115m per 100g (126yd per 3½oz), or any lightweight chunky (bulky) yarn
**M** – Cream – Loved x 1 ball
**C** – Black – Inspired x a very small amount
6mm (US 10) straight needles, 100g (3½oz) toy stuffing, 2 x 10mm toy eyes and washers

**SCRAP YARN MARKERS**
Colour **X** – Eye placement
Colour **Y** – Ear placement
Colour **Z** – Leg placement

**TENSION (GAUGE):** 16 sts x 20 rows = 10cm (4in)

**FINISHED SIZE:** 38 x 18 x 20cm (15 x 7 x 8in)

**TOP PIECE** – Make One
Cast on 3 stitches in M.
<u>Row 2</u> P all even rows unless otherwise stated. Even rows have been <u>underlined</u>.
**Row 3** *Kfb* all stitches (6 sts)
**Row 5** *Kfb, K1* all stitches (9 sts)
**Row 7** K
**Row 9** *Kfb, K2* all stitches (12 sts)
**Row 11** K
**Row 13** K
**Row 15** *Kfb, K1* all stitches (18 sts)
<u>Row 16</u> P [add colour **X** scrap yarn markers to the 7th and 13th stitches]
**Row 17** K
**Row 19** *Kfb, K2* all stitches (24 sts)
**Row 21** K
**Row 23** K
**Row 25** K [add colour **Y** scrap yarn markers to the 5th, 10th, 15th and 20th stitches]
**Row 27** K
**Row 29** K
**Row 31** *K2, K2tog* all stitches (18 sts)
**Row 33** *K1, K2tog* all stitches (12 sts)
**Row 35** K
**Row 37** *K2tog* all stitches (6 sts)
**Row 39** K
**Row 41** K
**Row 43** K1, Kfb, K1, Kfb, K2 (8 sts)
**Row 45** K
**Row 47** K1, Kfb, K3, Kfb, K2 (10 sts)

**Row 49** K
**Row 51** K1, Kfb, K5, Kfb, K2 (12 sts)
**Row 53** K1, Kfb, K7, Kfb, K2 (14 sts)
**Row 55** K1, Kfb, K9, Kfb, K2 (16 sts)
**Row 57** K1, Kfb, K11, Kfb, K2 (18 sts)
**Rows 59-66** Work in St st
**Row 67** *Kfb, K2* all stitches (24 sts)
**Row 69** K
**Row 71** K
**Row 73** K
**Row 75** *K2, K2tog* all stitches (18 sts)
**Row 77** *K1, K2tog* all stitches (12 sts)
**Row 79** *K2tog* all stitches (6 sts)
**Row 81** Cast (bind) off.

**UNDER PIECE** – Make One
Cast on 3 stitches in M.
**Row 2** P all even rows.
**Row 3** *Kfb* all stitches (6 sts)
**Row 5** *Kfb, K1* all stitches (9 sts)
**Row 7** K
**Row 9** *Kfb, K2* all stitches (12 sts)
**Rows 11-20** Work in St st
**Row 21** *Kfb, K3* all stitches (15 sts)
**Row 23** K
**Row 25** K
**Row 27** *Kfb, K4* all stitches (18 sts)
**Row 29** K
**Row 31** K
**Row 33** *Kfb, K2* all stitches (24 sts)
**Row 35** K
**Row 37** *Kfb, K3* all stitches (30 sts)
**Row 39** K [add colour **Z** scrap

yarn markers to the 9th, 14th, 17th and 22nd stitches]
**Row 41** *Kfb, K4* all stitches (36 sts)
**Row 43** K
**Row 45** K [add colour **Z** scrap yarn markers to the 11th, 17th, 21st and 27th stitches]
**Rows 47-62** Work in St st
**Row 63** K [add colour **Z** scrap yarn markers to the 11th, 17th, 21st and 27th stitches]
**Row 65** K
**Row 67** K
**Row 69** K [add colour **Z** scrap yarn markers to the 11th, 17th, 21st and 27th stitches]
**Row 71** *K4, K2tog* all stitches (30 sts)
**Row 73** *K3, K2tog* all stitches (24 sts)
**Row 75** *K2, K2tog* all stitches (18 sts)
**Row 77** *K1, K2tog* all stitches (12 sts)
**Row 79** *K2tog* all stitches (6 sts)
**Row 81** Cast (bind) off.

**EARS** – Make Four Pieces
Cast on 7 stitches in M.
**Row 2** P all even rows.
**Row 3** K
**Row 5** K1, SKP, K1, K2tog, K1 (5 sts)
**Row 7** Cast (bind) off.

## FRONT LEGS – Make Two

Cast on 18 stitches in M.
**Row 2** P all even rows.
**Rows 3-10** Work in St st
**Row 11** K6, *Kfb* six times, K6 (24 sts)
**Row 13** K
**Row 15** *K2, K2tog* all stitches (18 sts)
**Row 17** *K1, K2tog* all stitches (12 sts)
**Row 19** *K2tog* all stitches (6 sts)
Cut the yarn leaving a tail for sewing up. Thread it through the remaining six stitches and pull tightly.

## BACK LEGS – Make Two

Cast on 18 stitches in M.
**Row 2** P all even rows.
**Rows 3-6** Work in St st
**Row 7** K6, *Kfb* six times, K6 (24 sts)
**Row 9** K
**Row 11** *K2, K2tog* all stitches (18 sts)
**Row 13** *K1, K2tog* all stitches (12 sts)
**Row 15** *K2tog* all stitches (6 sts)
Cut the yarn leaving a tail for sewing up. Thread it through the remaining six stitches and pull tightly.

## TAIL – Make One

Cast on 6 stitches in M.
**Row 2** P all even rows.
**Rows 3-8** Work in St st
**Row 9** *K2tog* all stitches (3 sts)
Cut the yarn leaving a tail for sewing up. Thread it through the remaining three stitches and pull tightly.

## NOSE – Make One

Cast on 3 stitches in C.
**Row 2** P all even rows.
**Row 3** Kfb, Kfb, K1 (5 sts)
**Row 5** Cast (bind) off.

## SEWING UP

Weave in the loose ends. Take the top and under pieces and place the wrong sides together.

Sew up using a mattress stitch in M, leaving a hole for stuffing. Stuff the polar bear following the shape of the knit.

Take the 10mm toy eyes and place over the colour X scrap yarn markers. Remove the markers and secure the eyes with washers. Sew up the hole in the body using a mattress stitch in M.

Place the nose in the centre of the snout on the top piece of the bear, with the cast on edge of the nose sitting slightly above the cast on edge seam. Sew into place using C.

Take two ear pieces and place the wrong sides together. Sew up using a mattress stitch in M, leaving the cast on edges open. Stuff the ear. Repeat for the second ear. Place the first ear between the right-hand set of colour Y scrap yarn markers. Sew the cast on edges of the ear against the knit of the head using M. Repeat for the second ear, placing it between the left-hand set of colour Y scrap yarn markers; sew it into place using M. Remove the markers.

Sew up each leg from the thread-through end to the cast on edge using a mattress stitch in M. Leave the cast on edges open. Stuff each leg evenly. On the under piece find the set of colour Z scrap yarn markers that are closest to the cast on edge. There will be eight markers in total. Place the first front leg between the set of four markers on the right-hand side. Two will be on Row 39; the other two will be a few rows down on Row 45. Sew the cast on edge of the leg against the knit of the under piece using M. Then place the second front leg between the four colour Z scrap yarn markers on the left-hand side. Remove the markers and sew into place. Find the other set of colour Z scrap yarn markers; they will be closest to the cast (bound) off edge. Place the first back leg between the right-hand set of markers and sew into place. Then place the other leg between the left-hand set of markers and sew into place.

Sew the tail onto the back of the polar bear, against the cast (bound) off edge seam. Sew the cast on edge of the tail against the body of the polar bear using M. Weave in all the loose ends.

# TOUCAN

**MATERIALS**

Scheepjes Colour Crafter, 100% acrylic, 300m per 100g (328yd per 3½oz), or any DK yarn
A – Grey – 2019 Sint Niklaas x 1 ball
B – Black – 1002 Ede x 1 ball
C – Copper – 1711 Leeuwarden x 1 ball
D – White – 1001 Weert x 1 ball
M – Yellow – 1823 Coevorden x 1 ball

4mm (US 6) straight needles, stitch holder, a few handfuls of toy stuffing, 2 x 10mm toy eyes and washers

**SCRAP YARN MARKERS:** Colour Y – Wing placement
**TENSION (GAUGE):** 20 sts x 24 rows = 10cm (4in)
**FINISHED SIZE:** 32 x 8 x 8cm (12½ x 3¼ x 3¼in)

**TOP PIECE** – Make One
Cast on 3 stitches in B.
**Row 2** P
**Row 3** Kfb, Kfb, K1 (5 sts)
**Row 4** P
**Row 5** K2B, K1C, K2B
**Row 6** P2B, P1C, P2B
**Row 7** K2M, K1C, K2M
**Row 8** P2M, P1C, P2M
**Row 9** Kfb in M, K1M, K1C, Kfb in M, K1M (7 sts)
**Row 10** P3M, P1C, P3M
**Row 11** K3M, K1C, K3M
**Row 12** P3M, P1C, P3M
**Row 13** Kfb in M, Kfb in M, K1M, K1C, Kfb in M, Kfb in M, K1M (11 sts)
**Row 14** P5M, P1C, P5M
**Row 15** K5M, K1C, K5M
**Row 16** P5M, P1C, P5M
**Row 17** Kfb in M, K2M, Kfb in M, K1M, K1C, Kfb in M, K2M, Kfb in M, K1M (15 sts)
**Row 18** P7M, P1C, P7M
**Row 19** K7M, K1C, K7M
**Row 20** P7M, P1C, P7M
**Rows 21-30** Repeat Rows 19-20 five more times
**Row 31** K1M, SKP in M, K4M, K1C, K4M, K2tog in M, K1M (13 sts)
**Row 32** P6M, P1C, P6M
**Row 33** K all stitches in B
**Row 34** P all stitches in B
**Row 35** K5M, Kfb in B, Kfb in B, Kfb in B, K5M (16 sts)

**Row 36** P5M, P6B, P5M
**Row 37** K3M, K2tog in M, Kfb in B, K1B, Kfb in B, K1B, Kfb in B, K1B, SKP in M, K3M (17 sts)
**Row 38** P4M, P9B, P4M
**Row 39** K2M, K2tog in M, Kfb in B, K2B, Kfb in B, K2B, Kfb in B, K2B, SKP in M, K2M (18 sts)
**Row 40** Work all stitches in B from here. P
**Row 41** K
**Row 42** P all even rows from here.
**Row 43** K
**Row 45** K5, K2tog, K2, K2tog, K2, K2tog, K3 (15 sts)
**Row 47** K4, K2tog, K1, K2tog, K1, K2tog, K3 (12 sts)
**Row 49** K3, K2tog, K2tog, K2tog, K3 (9 sts)
**Row 51** K
**Row 53** K
**Row 55** *Kfb, K2* all stitches (12 sts)
**Row 57** Kfb, K to the last two stitches, Kfb, K1 (14 sts)
**Row 59** K
**Row 61** Kfb, K to the last two stitches, Kfb, K1 (16 sts)
**Row 63** K
**Row 65** Kfb, K to the last two stitches, Kfb, K1 (18 sts)
**Rows 67-76** Work in St st
**Row 77** *K1, K2tog* all stitches (12 sts)
**Row 79** *K2tog* all stitches (6 sts)
**Row 81** Cast (bind) off.

**UNDER PIECE** – Make One
Cast on 3 stitches in C.
**Row 2** P all even rows unless otherwise stated. P rows have been underlined.
**Row 3** Kfb, Kfb, K1 (5 sts)
**Row 5** K
**Row 7** Kfb, K2, Kfb, K1 (7 sts)
**Row 9** Kfb, K4, Kfb, K1 (9 sts)
**Row 11** K
**Row 13** Kfb, K6, Kfb, K1 (11 sts)
**Row 15** K
**Row 17** Kfb, K8, Kfb, K1 (13 sts)
**Rows 19-30** Work in St st
**Row 31** K1, SKP, K7, K2tog, K1 (11 sts)
**Row 33** K all stitches in B
<u>**Row 34**</u> P all stitches in B
**Row 35** Change to D, working all stitches in it until otherwise stated.
**Row 37** *Kfb, K1* four times, Kfb, Kfbf, K1 (18 sts)
**Row 39** K
**Row 41** *Kfb, K2* all stitches (24 sts)
**Row 43** K
**Row 45** *Kfb, K3* all stitches (30 sts)
**Row 47** K
**Row 49** K3B, K24D, K3B
<u>**Row 50**</u> P6B, P18D, P6B
**Row 51** K8B, K14D, P8B
<u>**Row 52**</u> P10B, P10D, P10B
**Row 53** K11B, K8D, K11B

**Row 54** P12B [add colour Y scrap yarn markers to the 2nd and 9th of these twelve stitches], P6D, P12B [add colour Y scrap yarn markers to the 4th and 11th of these twelve stitches]

**Row 55** Work all stitches in B from here. K

**Row 56** P

**Rows 57-72** Work in St st

**Row 73** *K3, K2tog* all stitches (24 sts)

**Row 75** *K2, K2tog* all stitches (18 sts)

**Row 77** *K1, K2tog* all stitches (12 sts)

**Row 79** *K2tog* all stitches (6 sts)

**Row 81** Cast (bind) off.

**WINGS** – Make Two
Cast on 12 stitches in B.

**Rows 2-8** *K2, P2* all stitches

**Row 9** *Kfb, K1, P2* all stitches (15 sts)

**Row 10** *K2, P3* all stitches

**Row 11** *P3, K2* all stitches (this row is intentional)

**Row 12** *P2, K3* all stitches

**Row 13** *P3, K2* all stitches

**Row 14** *P2, K3* all stitches

**Row 15** *P3, Kfb, K1* all stitches (18 sts)

**Row 16** *P3, K3* all stitches

**Row 17** *K3, P3* all stitches (this row is intentional)

**Row 18** *K3, P3* all stitches

**Row 19** *K3, P3* all stitches

**Row 20** *K3, P3* all stitches

**Row 21** *K3, P3* all stitches

**Row 22** *K3, P3* all stitches

**Row 23** *K1, K2tog, P1, P2tog* all stitches (12 sts)

**Row 24** *K2, P2* all stitches

**Row 25** *K2tog, P2tog* all stitches (6 sts)

**Row 26** *K1, P1* all stitches

**Row 27** Cast (bind) off.

**TAIL** – Make One
Cast on 12 stitches in B.

**Rows 2-12** *K2, P2* all stitches

**Row 13** *Kfb, K1, P2* all stitches (15 sts)

**Row 14** *K2, P3* all stitches

**Row 15** *K3, P2* all stitches

**Row 16** *K2, P3* all stitches

**Row 17** *K3, P2* all stitches

**Row 18** *Kfb, K1, P3* all stitches (18 sts)

**Rows 19-28** *K3, P3* all stitches

**Row 29** *K1, K2tog, P1, P2tog* all stitches (12 sts)

**Row 30** *K2, P2* all stitches

**Row 31** *K2tog, P2tog* all stitches (6 sts)

**Row 32** *K1, P1* all stitches

**Row 33** Cast (bind) off.

**FEET** – Make Two
Cast on 3 stitches in A.

**Row 2** K

**Row 3** *Kfb* all stitches (6 sts)

**Row 4** K

**Row 5** K

**Row 6** K

**Row 7** K2, TURN, placing the remaining four stitches on a holder to be worked later.

**Row 8** K

**Row 9** K

**Row 10** K

**Row 11** K

**Row 12** K

**Row 13** Cast (bind) off.
Move 2 stitches from the holder onto the left-hand needle ready to be worked from Row 7.

**Row 7** Reattach the yarn and K

**Row 8** K

**Row 9** K

**Row 10** K

**Row 11** K

**Row 12** K

**Row 13** Cast (bind) off.
Move the remaining 2 stitches from the holder onto the left-hand needle ready to be worked from Row 7.

**Row 7** Reattach the yarn and K

**Row 8** K

**Row 9** K

**Row 10** K

**Row 11** K

**Row 12** K

**Row 13** Cast (bind) off.

**SEWING UP**
Weave in the loose ends. Place the top and under pieces the wrong sides together. Sew up using a mattress stitch in B, leaving a hole for stuffing. Stuff the toucan following the shape of the knit.

Place the 10mm eyes in the centre of the yellow knit sections after the beak on the top piece of the toucan. Secure into place with washers. Sew up the hole in the body using a mattress stitch in B.

Place a wing between the right-hand set of colour Y scrap yarn markers. Sew the cast on edge of the wing against the knit of the body using B. Place the other wing between the left-hand set of colour Y scrap yarn markers and sew into place using B. Remove the markers.

Place each foot on the under piece of the toucan, 3cm (1¼in) from the cast (bound) off edge seam. Sew the cast on edges of the feet against the knit of the toucan using A, leaving a gap of 0.5cm (¼in) in the centre between them.

Place the tail on the centre of the top piece of the toucan, just above the cast (bound) off edge seam. Sew into place using B. Weave in the loose ends.

# MEERKAT

**TOP PIECE** – Make One
Cast on 3 stitches in M.
**Row 2** P all even rows unless
  otherwise stated. P rows have
  been <u>underlined</u>.
**Row 3** *Kfb* all stitches (6 sts)
**Row 5** K
**Row 7** K1, Kfb, K1, Kfb, K2 (8 sts)
**Row 9** K
**Row 11** *Kfb, K1* all stitches (12 sts)
**Row 13** Kfb in M, K1M, K2C, Kfb
  in M, K1M, Kfb in M, K1M, K2C,
  Kfb in M, K1M (16 sts)
<u>**Row 14**</u> P3M, P3C, P4M, P3C, P3M
**Row 15** Kfb in M, K1M, K5C, K2M,
  K5C, Kfb in M, K1M (18 sts)
<u>**Row 16**</u> P3M, P5C, P2M, P5C, P3M
**Row 17** Kfb in M, K2M, K3C, K2tog
  in C, Kfb in M, Kfb in M, SKP in C,
  K3C, Kfb in M, K2M (20 sts)
<u>**Row 18**</u> P4M, P4C, P4M, P4C, P4M
**Row 19** Work all stitches in M
  from here. Kfb, K6, Kfb, K2, Kfb,
  K7, Kfb, K1 (24 sts)
**Row 21** K
**Row 23** K
**Row 25** K [add colour Y scrap
  yarn markers to the 2nd, 8th,
  15th and 21st of these stitches]
**Row 27** K
**Row 29** *K4, K2tog* all stitches
  (20 sts)
**Row 31** *K3, K2tog* all stitches
  (16 sts)
**Row 33** *K2, K2tog* all stitches
  (12 sts)

**Row 35** *K1, K2tog* all stitches
  (8 sts)
**Rows 37-42** Work in St st
**Row 43** Kfb, K5, Kfb, K1 (10 sts)
**Row 45** K
**Row 47** Kfb, K7, Kfb, K1 (12 sts)
**Row 49** K
**Row 51** Kfb, K9, Kfb, K1 (14 sts)
**Row 53-60** Work in St st
**Row 61** Kfb, K11, Kfb, K1 (16 sts)
**Rows 63-68** Work in St st
**Row 69** Kfb, K13, Kfb, K1 (18 sts)
**Rows 71-90** Work in St st
**Row 91** *K1, K2tog* all stitches
  (12 sts)
**Row 93** *K2tog* all stitches (6 sts)
**Row 95** Cast (bind) off.

**UNDER PIECE** – Make One
Cast on 3 stitches in M.
**Row 2** P all even rows.
**Row 3** *Kfb* all stitches (6 sts)
**Rows 5-12** Work in St st
**Row 13** *Kfb, K1* all stitches
  (9 sts)
**Row 15** K
**Row 17** *Kfb, K2* all stitches (12 sts)
**Row 19** K
**Row 21** *Kfb, K3* all stitches (15 sts)
**Row 23** K
**Row 25** *Kfb, K4* all stitches
  (18 sts)
**Row 27** *K1, K2tog* all stitches
  (12 sts)
**Row 29** *K2tog* all stitches (6 sts)
**Row 31** K

**Row 33** Kfb, K3, Kfb, K1 (8 sts)
**Row 35** *Kfb, K1* all stitches
  (12 sts)
**Row 37** K
**Row 39** *Kfb, K1* all stitches
  (18 sts)
**Row 41** K
**Row 43** *Kfb, K2* all stitches
  (24 sts)
**Rows 45-50** Work in St st
**Row 51** *Kfb, K7* all stitches
  (27 sts)
**Rows 53-56** Work in St st
**Row 57** *Kfb, K8* all stitches
  (30 sts)
**Rows 59-86** Work in St st
**Row 87** *K3, K2tog* all stitches
  (24 sts)
**Row 89** *K2, K2tog* all stitches
  (18 sts)
**Row 91** *K1, K2tog* all stitches
  (12 sts)
**Row 93** *K2tog* all stitches
  (6 sts)
**Row 95** Cast (bind) off.

**BACK LEGS** – Make Two
Cast on 18 stitches in M.
**Row 2** P all even rows.
**Row 3** *Kfb, K2* all stitches (24 sts)
**Rows 5-12** Work in St st
**Row 13** *K2, K2tog* all stitches
  (18 sts)
**Rows 15-26** Work in St st
**Row 27** *K1, K2tog* all stitches
  (12 sts)

**Row 29** *K2tog* all stitches (6 sts)
Cut the yarn leaving a tail for sewing up. Thread it through the remaining six stitches and pull tightly. Sew up from the thread-through end to cast on edge using a mattress stitch.

**FRONT LEGS** – Make Two
Cast on 18 stitches in M.
**Row 2** P all even rows.
**Rows 3-10** Work in St st
**Row 11** *K4, K2tog* all stitches (15 sts)
**Row 13** K
**Row 15** K
**Row 17** *K3, K2tog* all stitches (12 sts)
**Row 19** K
**Row 21** K
**Row 23** *K2tog* all stitches (6 sts)
Cut the yarn leaving a tail for sewing up. Thread it through the remaining six stitches and pull tightly. Sew up from the thread-through end to cast on edge using a mattress stitch.

**TAIL** – Make One
Cast on 15 stitches in M.
**Row 2** P all even rows.
**Rows 3-26** Work in St st
**Row 27** *K3, K2tog* all stitches (12 sts)
**Row 29** K
**Row 31** *K2, K2tog* all stitches (9 sts)
**Row 33** K
**Row 35** *K1, K2tog* all stitches (6 sts)
Cut the yarn leaving a tail for sewing up. Thread it through the remaining six stitches and pull tightly. Sew up from the thread-through end to cast on edge using a mattress stitch in M.

**EARS** – Make Four Pieces
Cast on 8 stitches in C.
**Row 2** P all even rows.
**Row 3** K
**Row 5** K
**Row 7** K1, SKP, K2, K2tog, K1 (6 sts)
**Row 9** Cast (bind) off.

**SEWING UP**
Weave in the loose ends. Take the top and under pieces and place the wrong sides together. Sew up using a mattress stitch in M, leaving a hole for stuffing. Stuff the meerkat following the shape of the knit. The neck should have very little stuffing; this allows the face to naturally drop forwards. Once the meerkat is stuffed, it will look like a bowling pin.

Take two 10mm toy eyes and place one in the centre of each C colour change on the top piece of the meerkat. Secure the eyes with washers. Place the third 10mm eye in the centre of the snout on the top piece to create the nose. Secure with a washer. Sew up the hole in the body using a mattress stitch in M. Add a stitch under the head, sewing the neck to the underside. This will pull the head into place.

Take two ear pieces and place the wrong sides together. Sew up using a mattress stitch in C. Leave the cast on edges open. Do not stuff the ear. Repeat for the second ear. Place the first ear between the right-hand set of colour Y scrap yarn markers. Sew the cast on edge of the ear against the knit of the head. Repeat for the second ear, placing it between the left-hand set of markers and sewing into place. Remove the markers.

Stuff each leg piece evenly. Take the back legs and place them 2cm (¾in) from the cast (bound) off edge seam, leaving a gap of 4cm (1½in) between them. They will sit on the sides of the meerkat, facing slightly outwards. Sew the cast on edges of the legs against the knit of the body using M.

Place the front legs 14cm (5½in) from the cast (bound) off edge seam, leaving a gap of 4cm (1½in) in the centre between them. Sew the cast on edges of the legs against the knit of the body using M.

Stuff the tail and place it 3cm (1¼in) from the cast (bound) off edge seam. Sew the cast on edge into place against the knit of the body using M. Weave in the loose ends.

# KILLER WHALE

**MATERIALS**

Bobbiny 3mm Junior Cord, recycled cotton, 100m per 100g (109yd per 3½oz), or any corded yarn (whales are not fluffy)
**M** – Black x 2 balls; **C** – Cream x 1 ball
7mm (US 10½) straight needles, stitch holder, 150g (5oz) toy stuffing, 2 x 15mm toy eyes and washers

**SCRAP YARN MARKERS**

Colour **X** – Eye placement
Colour **Y** – Side fin placement
Colour **Z** – Top fin placement

**TENSION (GAUGE):** 10 sts x 13 rows = 10cm (4in)

**FINISHED SIZE:** 78 x 42 x 28cm (30¾ x 16½ x 11in)

**TOP PIECE** – Make One
Cast on 6 stitches in M.
**Row 2** P all even rows until Row 10.
**Row 3** *Kfb, K1* all stitches (9 sts)
**Row 5** *Kfb, K2* all stitches (12 sts)
**Row 7** *Kfb, K3* all stitches (15 sts)
**Row 9** *Kfb, K4* all stitches (18 sts)
**Row 10** P [add colour X scrap yarn markers to the 3rd and 16th sts]
**Rows 11–12** Work in St st
*Tip: use the intarsia technique when changing colour (see page 5). You can carry the yarn but additional yarn may be required.*
**Row 13** K2M, K2C, K10M, K2C, K2M
**Row 14** P2M, P2C, P10M, P2C, P2M
**Row 15** Kfb in M, K1M, Kfb in C, K2C, K8M, K1C, Kfb in C, K1C, Kfb in M, K1M (22 sts)
**Row 16** P3M, P4C, P8M, P4C, P3M
**Row 17** K3M, K2C, Kfb in C, K1C, K8M, Kfb in C, K3C, K3M (24 sts)
**Row 18** P3M, P5C, P8M, P5C, P3M
**Row 19** Kfb in M, K2M, K5C, K8M, K5C, K1M, Kfb in M, K1M (26 sts)
**Row 20** P4M, P5C, P8M, P5C, P4M
**Row 21** K4M, K5C, K8M, K5C, K4M
**Row 22** P4M, P5C, P8M, P5C, P4M
**Row 23** Kfb in M, K1M, Kfb in M, K1M, K2C, K2tog in C, K1C, K8M, K1C, SKP in C, K2C, Kfb in M, K1M, Kfb in M, K1M (28 sts)
**Row 24** P6M, P4C, P8M, P4C, P6M
**Row 25** Kfb in M, K5M, K1C, K2tog in C, K1C, K8M, K1C, SKP in C, K1C, K4M, Kfb in M, K1M (28 sts)

**Row 26** P7M [add a colour Y scrap yarn marker to the 2nd of these seven stitches], P3C, P8M, P3C, P7M [add a colour Y scrap yarn maker to the 6th of these seven stitches]
**Row 27** Work all stitches in M until otherwise stated. Kfb, K to the last two stitches, Kfb, K1 (30 sts)
**Row 28** P
**Rows 29–32** Work in St st
**Row 33** K [add colour Y scrap yarn markers to the 2nd and 29th of these stitches]
**Row 34** P
**Rows 35–48** Work in St st
**Row 49** K [add colour Z scrap yarn markers to the 13th and 18th of these stitches]
**Row 50** P
**Row 51** K2C, K26M, K2C
**Row 52** P2C, P26M, P2C
**Rows 53–54** Repeat Rows 51–52.
**Row 55** K3C, K24M, K3C
**Row 56** P3C, P24M, P3C
**Rows 57–58** Repeat Rows 55–56.
**Row 59** K5C, K20M, K5C
**Row 60** P7C, P16M [add colour Z scrap yarn markers to the 6th and 11th of these sixteen stitches], P7C
**Row 61** K9C, K12M, K9C
**Row 62** P11C, P8M, P11C
**Row 63** K12C, K6M, K12C
**Row 64** P12C, P6M, P12C
**Rows 65–66** Repeat Rows 63–64.
**Row 67** K9C, K2tog in C, K1C,

K6M, K1C, SKP in C, K9C (28 sts)
**Row 68** P11C, P6M, P11C
**Row 69** K11C, K6M, K11C
**Row 70** P11C, P6M, P11C
**Row 71** K2M, K6C, K2tog in C, K1C, K6M, K1C, SKP in C, K6C, K2M (26 sts)
**Row 72** P2M, P8C, P6M, P8C, P2M
**Row 73** Kfb in M, K1M, K5C, K2tog in C, K1C, K6M, K1C, SKP in C, K5C, Kfb in M, K1M (26 sts)
**Row 74** P4M, P6C, P6M, P6C, P4M
**Row 75** Kfb in M, K3M, K3C, K2tog in C, K1C, K6M, K1C, K2tog in C, K3C, K2M, Kfb in M, K1M (26 sts)
**Row 76** P5M, P5C, P6M, P5C, P5M
**Row 77** K5M, K2C, K2tog in C, K1C, K6M, K1C, SKP in C, K2C, K5M (24 sts)
**Row 78** P5M, P4C, P6M, P4C, P5M
**Row 79** K5M, K1C, K2tog in C, K1C, K6M, K1C, SKP in C, K1C, K5M (22 sts)
**Row 80** P5M, P3C, P6M, P3C, P5M
**Row 81** K5M, K2tog in C, K1C, K6M, K1C, SKP in C, K5M (20 sts)
**Row 82** Work all stitches in M from here. P
**Row 83** K4, SKP, K8, K2tog, K4 (18 sts)
**Row 84** P all even rows from here unless otherwise stated.
**Row 85** K
**Row 87** K3, SKP, K8, K2tog, K3 (16 sts)
**Row 89** K
**Row 91** K2, SKP, K8, K2tog, K2 (14 sts)
**Row 93** K

**Row 95** K1, SKP, K8, K2tog, K1 (12 sts)
**Rows 97-108** Work in St st
**Row 109** Kfb, Kfb, K to the last three stitches, Kfb, Kfb, K1 (16 sts)
**Row 111** Repeat Row 109 (20 sts)
**Row 113** Repeat Row 109 (24 sts)
**Row 115** K
**Row 117** Kfb, K to the last two stitches, Kfb, K1 (26 sts)
**Row 119** K

*Right Side of Tail Fin*
**Row 121** K10, K2tog, K1 (12 sts), TURN, placing remaining 13 stitches on a holder to be worked later.
**Row 122** P the 12 stitches
**Row 123** K
**Row 124** P
**Row 125** Cast (bind) off.

*Left Side of Tail Fin*
Move the 13 stitches from the holder onto the left-hand needle ready to be worked from Row 121.
**Row 121** Reattach the yarn and K1, SKP, K10 (12 sts)
**Row 122** P
**Row 123** K
**Row 124** P
**Row 125** Cast (bind) off.

**UNDER PIECE** - Make One
Cast on 6 stitches in C.
**Row 2** P all even rows unless otherwise stated.
**Row 3** *Kfb, K1* all stitches (9 sts)
**Row 5** *Kfb, K2* all stitches (12 sts)
**Row 7** *Kfb, K3* all stitches (15 sts)
**Row 9** *Kfb, K4* all stitches (18 sts)
**Row 11** K
**Row 13** K
**Row 15** *Kfb, K5* all stitches (21 sts)
**Row 17** *Kfb, K6* all stitches (24 sts)
**Row 19** K1, SKP, K to the last three stitches, K2tog, K1 (22 sts)
**Row 21** K
**Row 23** Repeat Row 19 (20 sts)
**Row 25** K
**Row 27** Repeat Row 19 (18 sts)
**Rows 29-76** Work in St st
**Row 77** K1, SKP, K to the last three stitches, K2tog, K1 (16 sts)
**Row 79** K
**Row 81-92** Repeat Rows 77-80

three more times. (10 sts)
**Rows 93-106** Work in St st
**Row 107** Kfb, K to the last two stitches, Kfb, K1 (12 sts)
**Row 109** Kfb, Kfb, K to the last three stitches, Kfb, Kfb, K1 (16 sts)
**Row 111** Repeat Row 109 (20 sts)
**Row 113** Repeat Row 109 (24 sts)
**Row 115** K
**Row 117** Kfb, K to the last two stitches, Kfb, K1 (26 sts)
**Row 119** K

*Right Side of Tail Fin*
**Row 121** K10, K2tog, K1 (12 sts), TURN, placing remaining 13 stitches on a holder to be worked later.
**Row 122** P the 12 stitches
**Row 123** K
**Row 124** P
**Row 125** Cast (bind) off.

*Left Side of Tail Fin*
Move the 13 stitches from the holder onto the left-hand needle ready to be worked from Row 121.
**Row 121** Reattach the yarn and K1, SKP, K10 (12 sts)
**Row 122** P
**Row 123** K
**Row 124** P
**Row 125** Cast (bind) off.

**TOP FIN - Piece One** - Make One
Cast on 12 stitches in M.
**Row 2** P all even rows.
**Row 3** K
**Row 5** K1, SKP, K9 (11 sts)
**Row 7** K1, SKP, K8 (10 sts)
**Row 9** K1, SKP, K5, Kfb, K1 (10 sts)
**Row 11** K1, SKP, K7 (9 sts)
**Row 13** K1, SKP, K4, Kfb, K1 (9 sts)
**Row 15** K1, SKP, K6 (8 sts)
**Row 17** K1, SKP, K3, Kfb, K1 (8 sts)
**Row 19** K1, SKP, SKP, K3 (6 sts)
**Row 21** Cast (bind) off.

**TOP FIN - Piece Two** - Make One
Cast on 12 stitches in M.
**Row 2** P all even rows.
**Row 3** K
**Row 5** K9, K2tog, K1 (11 sts)
**Row 7** K8, K2tog, K1 (10 sts)
**Row 9** K1, Kfb, K5, K2tog, K1 (10 sts)

**Row 11** K7, K2tog, K1 (9 sts)
**Row 13** K1, Kfb, K4, K2tog, K1 (9 sts)
**Row 15** K6, K2tog, K1 (8 sts)
**Row 17** K1, Kfb, K3, K2tog, K1 (8 sts)
**Row 19** K3, K2tog, K2tog, K1 (6 sts)
**Row 21** Cast (bind) off.

**SIDE FINS** - Make Four Pieces
Cast on 8 stitches in M.
**Row 2** P all even rows.
**Row 3** K
**Row 5** K1, Kfb, K3, Kfb, K2 (10 sts)
**Rows 7-14** Work in St st
**Row 15** K1, SKP, K4, K2tog, K1 (8 sts)
**Row 17** K1, SKP, K2, K2tog, K1 (6 sts)
**Row 19** K1, SKP, K2tog, K1 (4 sts)
**Row 21** Cast (bind) off.

**SEWING UP**
Weave in the loose ends. Take the top and under pieces and place the wrong sides together. Sew up using a mattress stitch in M, leaving a hole for stuffing. Stuff the whale following the shape of the knit. Take the toy eyes and place over the colour X scrap yarn markers. Remove the markers and secure with washers. Sew up the hole in the body.

Take two of the side fin pieces and place the wrong sides together. Sew up using a mattress stitch in M, leaving the cast on edges open. Stuff the fin. Repeat for the second side fin. Place the first side fin between the two colour Y scrap yarn markers on the right-hand side of the whale. Sew the cast on edges of the fin against the body of the whale. Repeat for the other side fin, placing it between the two colour Y scrap yarn markers on the left-hand side and sewing into place.

Take the top fin pieces and place the wrong sides together. Sew up using a mattress stitch in M, leaving the cast on edges open. Stuff the fin. Find the four colour Z scrap yarn markers and place the top fin between them. Sew the cast on edges of the fin against the body of the whale. Remove all the markers and weave in the loose ends.

# CHICKENS

## MATERIALS

Scheepjes Colour Crafter, 100% acrylic, 300m per 100g (328yd per 3½oz), or any DK yarn (M will be different for each of the three chickens)
**M** - Gold - 1709 Burum x 1 ball
  - White - 1001 Weert x 1 ball
  - Black - 1002 Ede x 1 ball
**C** - Oatmeal - 1710 Ermelo x 1 ball

**D** - Red - 1010 Amsterdam x 1 ball
4mm (US 6) straight needles, a handful of toy stuffing

**TENSION (GAUGE):** 20 sts x 24 rows = 10cm (4in)

**FINISHED SIZE:** 15 x 12 x 8cm (6 x 4¾ x 3¼in)

**TOP PIECE** – Make One
Cast on 3 stitches in C.
**Row 2** P all even rows.
**Row 3** Kfb, Kfb, K1 (5 sts)
**Row 5** K
**Row 7** Change to M, working all stitches in it from here. K1, Kfb, Kfb, K2 (7 sts)
**Row 9** K2, Kfb, Kfb, K3 (9 sts)
**Row 11** Kfb, K2, Kfb, Kfb, K2, Kfb, K1 (13 sts)
**Row 13** K
**Row 15** K3, K2tog, K8 (12 sts)
**Row 17** *K2, K2tog* all stitches (9 sts)
**Row 19** *K1, K2tog* all stitches (6 sts)
**Rows 21-32** Work in St st
**Row 33** Kfb, K3, Kfb, K1 (8 sts)
**Row 35** K
**Row 37** Kfb, K5, Kfb, K1 (10 sts)
**Rows 39-46** Work in St st
**Row 47** K1, SKP, K4, K2tog, K1 (8 sts)
**Row 49** K1, SKP, K2, K2tog, K1 (6 sts)
**Row 51** K
**Row 53** K1, SKP, K2tog, K1 (4 sts)
**Rows 55-58** Work in St st
**Row 59** Cast (bind) off.

**UNDER PIECE** – Make One
Cast on 3 stitches in C.
**Row 2** P all even rows
**Row 3** Kfb, Kfb, K1 (5 sts)

**Row 5** K
**Row 7** Change to M, working all stitches in it from here. K2, Kfb, K2 (6 sts)
**Rows 9-14** Work in St st
**Row 15** *Kfb, K1* all stitches (9 sts)
**Row 17** *Kfb, K2* all stitches (12 sts)
**Row 19** K
**Row 21** *Kfb, K3* all stitches (15 sts)
**Row 23** K
**Row 25** *Kfb, K4* all stitches (18 sts)
**Row 27** *Kfb, K5* all stitches (21 sts)
**Row 29** *Kfb, K6* all stitches (24 sts)
**Row 31** K
**Row 33** *Kfb, K7* all stitches (27 sts)
**Row 35** K
**Row 37** *Kfb, K8* all stitches (30 sts)
**Rows 39-44** Work in St st
**Row 45** *K3, K2tog* all stitches (24 sts)
**Row 47** *K2, K2tog* all stitches (18 sts)
**Row 49** *K1, K2tog* all stitches (12 sts)
**Row 51** *K2tog* all stitches (6 sts)
**Row 53** K1, SKP, K2tog, K1 (4 sts)
**Row 55** K
**Row 57** K
**Row 59** Cast (bind) off.

**COMB** – Make One
Cast on 8 stitches in D.
**Row 2** K
**Row 3** K
**Row 4** K

**Row 5** K2, TURN, hold the remaining 6 stitches on the left-hand needle, but do not work them.
**Row 6** K the two stitches after the turn.
**Row 7** K2tog (1 st)
Cut the yarn leaving a small tail, thread it through the remaining stitch and weave in the loose end.
Reattach the yarn and repeat
**Rows 5-7** on the next two stitches.
Reattach the yarn and repeat
**Rows 5-7** on the next two stitches.
Reattach the yarn and repeat
**Rows 5-7** on the last two stitches.

**WATTLE** – Make Two
Cast on 4 stitches in D.
**Row 2** K
**Row 3** K
**Row 4** K
**Row 5** SKP, K2tog (2 sts)
Cut the yarn leaving a small tail, thread it through the remaining two stitches and pull tightly.

**WINGS** – Make Two
Cast on 13 stitches in M.
**Row 2** *P1, K1* six times, P1
**Row 3** *K1, P1* six times, K1
**Row 4** *P1, K1* six times, P1
**Row 5** *K1, P1* six times, K1
**Row 6** *P1, K1* six times, P1

**Row 7** *K1, P1* six times, K1
**Row 8** *P1, K1* six times, P1
**Row 9** K1, SKP, SKP, K3tog, K2tog, K2tog, K1 (7 sts)
**Row 10** P
**Row 11** Cast (bind) off.

LEGS – Make Two
Cast on 12 stitches in M.
**Row 2** P all even rows unless otherwise stated.
**Row 3** K
**Row 5** K
**Row 7** K
**Row 9** Change to C, working all stitches in it from here. *K2, K2tog* all stitches (9 sts)
**Row 11** K
**Row 13** K
**Row 15** K4, Kfb, Kfb, Kfb, cast (bind) off the last two stitches (10 sts)
**Row 16** Reattach the yarn and P all stitches
**Row 17** K2, TURN, hold the remaining 8 stitches on the left-hand needle, but do not work them.
**Row 18** P the two stitches after the turn.
**Row 19** K2tog (1 st)
Cut the yarn leaving a small tail. Thread it through the remaining stitch and pull tightly.
Reattach the yarn to the first of the 8 stitches on the left-hand needle, ready to work from Row 17.
**Row 17** Cast (bind) off 2 stitches, K1. You'll now have two stitches on the right-hand needle including the stitch just cast (bound) off. Turn the work again, using the same technique as the first turn, leaving 4 stitches on the left-hand needle.
**Row 18** P the two stitches after the turn.
**Row 19** K2tog (1 st)
Cut the yarn leaving a small tail. Thread it through the remaining stitch and pull tightly. Reattach the yarn, ready to work from Row 17.
**Row 17** K2. Turn the work again, using the same technique as the first turn, leaving the remaining

2 stitches on the left-hand needle.
**Row 18** P the two stitches after the turn.
**Row 19** K2tog (1 st)
Cut the yarn leaving a small tail. Thread it through the remaining stitch and pull tightly.
Reattach the yarn, ready to work from Row 17.
**Row 17** K the two stitches (these are the last two stitches on the needle)
**Row 18** P the two stitches
**Row 19** K2tog (1 st)
Cut the yarn leaving a small tail. Thread it through the remaining stitch and pull tightly.

SEWING UP

Weave in the loose ends. Take the top and under pieces of the chicken and place the wrong sides together. Sew up using a mattress stitch in M, leaving a hole for stuffing. Stuff the chicken evenly following the shape of the knit. Sew up the hole in the body.
Place the comb in the centre of the top piece of the chicken, 2.5cm (1in) from the cast on edge. Sew the cast on edge of the comb onto the head using D. Place the wattles on the under piece of the chicken, 2cm (¾in) from the cast on edge. Leave a gap of 0.5cm (¼in) between them. Sew into place using D.

Embroider a line in the centre of the side of the chicken's head, 2.5cm (1in) from the cast on edge. For the gold and white chickens use the black DK yarn. For the black chicken use the oatmeal DK yarn. The line should measure 0.8cm (¼–⅜in). Push the line down to create a sleepy eye and add a small stitch in the centre to secure it. Repeat for the eye on the other side of the chicken's head.
Place a wing on one side of the chicken, 8cm (3¼in) from the cast on edge and 4cm (1½in) from the cast (bound) off edge. The cast on edge of the wing should sit along the sewing up seam on the body. Sew into place using M. Sew the cast (bound) off edge of the wing into place against the body of the chicken. Repeat for the second wing on the other side of the chicken.
Sew up the legs from the cast (bound) off edge to the cast on edge using a mattress stitch. Stuff each leg following the shape of the knit. The bottom of the leg will be open, showing the stuffing. You could add a small circle of felt and sew it into place to cover up the hole. Place the legs directly under the centre of the wings, on the underside of the body. Leave a gap of 1cm (⅜in) in the centre between them. Sew into place using M. Weave in the loose ends.

# RACCOON

## MATERIALS
Scheepjes Colour Crafter, 100% acrylic, 300m per 100g (328yd per 3½oz), or any DK yarn
M - Grey - 2019 Sint Niklaas x 1 ball
B - Black - 1002 Ede x 1 ball
C - White - 1001 Weert x 1 ball
4mm (US 6) straight needles, 30g (1oz) toy stuffing, 2 x 15mm toy eyes and washers

## SCRAP YARN MARKERS
Colour X - Eye placement
Colour Y - Ear placement

**TENSION (GAUGE):** 20 sts x 24 rows = 10cm (4in)

**FINISHED SIZE:** 18 x 31 x 18cm (7 x 12¼ x 7in)

When changing colour, you can either use the intarsia technique (see page 5) or carry the yarn.

**TOP PIECE** - Make One
Cast on 3 stitches in C.
**Row 2** P
**Row 3** *Kfb* all stitches (6 sts)
**Row 4** P
**Row 5** K1, Kfb, K1, Kfb, K2 (8 sts)
**Row 6** P
**Row 7** K
**Row 8** P
**Row 9** K1C, Kfb in C, K1C, K2M, Kfb in C, K2C (10 sts)
**Row 10** P4C, P2M, P4C
**Row 11** K1C, Kfb in C, Kfb in C, K1C, K2M, Kfb in C, Kfb in C, K2C (14 sts)
**Row 12** P6C, P2M, P6C
**Row 13** K2B, Kfb in C, K1C, Kfb in C, K1C, K2M, Kfb in C, K1C, Kfb in C, K1C, K2B (18 sts)
**Row 14** P4B, P4C, P2M, P4C, P4B
**Row 15** K1B, Kfb in B, Kfb in B, K3B, K2C, K2M, K2C, K2B, Kfb in B, Kfb in B, K2B (22 sts)
**Row 16** P10B, P2M, P10B
**Row 17** K10B [add a colour X scrap yarn marker to the 7th of these ten stitches], K2M, K10B [add a colour X scrap yarn marker to the 4th of these ten stitches]
**Row 18** P10B, P2M, P10B
**Row 19** K1B, Kfb in B, K8B, K2M, K8B, Kfb in B, K1B (24 sts)
**Row 20** P11B, P2M, P11B
**Row 21** K3C, K7B, K1C, K2M, K1C, K7B, K3C
**Row 22** P5C, P5B, P1C, P2M, P1C, P5B, P5C
**Row 23** K7C, K2B, K2C, K2M, K2C, K2B, K7C
**Row 24** P11C, P2M, P11C
**Row 25** K3M, K8C, K2M, K8C, K3M
**Row 26** P6M, P5C, P2M, P5C, P6M
**Row 27** K9M, K2C, K2M, K2C, K9M
**Row 28** Work all stitches in M from here. P
**Row 29** K [add colour Y scrap yarn markers to the 4th, 10th, 15th and 21st stitches]
**Row 30** P all even rows from here.
**Row 31** K
**Row 33** K
**Row 35** *K6, K2tog* all sts (21 sts)
**Row 37** *K5, K2tog* all sts (18 sts)
**Row 39** *K4, K2tog* all sts (15 sts)
**Row 41** *K3, K2tog* all sts (12 sts)
**Row 43** *K2, K2tog* all sts (9 sts)
**Rows 45-64** Work in St st
**Row 65** *Kfb, K2* all sts (12 sts)
**Row 67** K
**Row 69** K
**Row 71** *Kfb, K3* all sts (15 sts)
**Rows 73-82** Work in St st
**Row 83** *K3, K2tog* all sts (12 sts)
**Row 85** *K2, K2tog* all sts (9 sts)
**Row 87** *K1, K2tog* all sts (6 sts)
**Row 91** Cast (bind) off.

**UNDER PIECE** - Make One
Cast on 3 stitches in C.
**Row 2** P all even rows until stated.
**Row 3** *Kfb* all stitches (6 sts)
**Row 5** *Kfb, K1* all stitches (9 sts)
**Row 7** K
**Row 9** *Kfb, K2* all stitches (12 sts)
**Row 11** *Kfb, K3* all stitches (15 sts)
**Row 13** *Kfb, K4* all stitches (18 sts)
**Row 15** *Kfb, K5* all stitches (21 sts)
**Row 17** *Kfb, K6* all stitches (24 sts)
**Rows 19-24** Work in St st
**Row 25** K2M, K20C, K2M
**Row 26** P3M, P18C, P3M
**Row 27** K3M, K18C, K3M
**Row 28** P3M, P18C, P3M
**Row 29** K2M, SKP in M, K16C, K2tog in M, K2M (22 sts)
**Row 30** P3M, P16C, P3M
**Row 31** K2M, SKP in M, K6C, K2tog in C, K6C, K2tog in M, K2M (19 sts)
**Row 32** P3M, P13C, P3M
**Row 33** K3M, K5C, K2tog in C, K6C, K3M (18 sts)
**Row 34** P3M, P12C, P3M
**Row 35** K3M, *Kfb in C, K1C* six times, K3M (24 sts)
**Row 36** P4M, P16C, P4M
**Row 37** K5M, K14C, K5M
**Row 38** P6M, P12C, P6M
**Row 39** K6M, Kfb in C, K3C, Kfb in C, K3C, Kfb in C, K3C, K6M (27 sts)
**Row 40** P7M, P13C, P7M
**Row 41** K6M, Kfb in M, K4C, Kfb in C, K4C, Kfb in C, K2C, K8M (30 sts)
**Row 42** P8M, P14C, P8M

**Row 43** K8M, K14C, K8M
**Row 44** P8M, P14C, P8M
**Row 45** K6M, Kfb in M, K1M, K4C, Kfb in C, K5C, Kfb in C, K2C, K9M (33 sts)
**Row 46** P9M, P14C, P10M
**Row 47** K6M, Kfb in M, K3M, K3C, Kfb in C, K6C, Kfb in C, K2C, K10M (36 sts)
**Row 48** P11M, P14C, P11M
**Row 49** K6M, Kfb in M, K5M, K2C, Kfb in C, K7C, Kfb in C, K1C, K12M (39 sts)
**Row 50** P14M, P11C, P14M
**Row 51** K6M, Kfb in M, K8M, Kfb in C, K7C, K1M, Kfb in M, K14M (42 sts)
**Row 52** P19M, P4C, P19M
**Row 53** Work all stitches in M from here. K6, Kfb, K9, Kfb, K9, Kfb, K15 (45 sts)
**Row 54** P all even rows from here.
**Row 55** K6, Kfb, K10, Kfb, K10, Kfb, K16 (48 sts)
**Row 57** *Kfb, K7* all sts (54 sts)
**Row 59** *Kfb, K8* all sts (60 sts)
**Rows 61-80** Work in St st
**Row 81** *K3, K2tog* all sts (48 sts)
**Row 83** *K2, K2tog* all sts (36 sts)
**Row 85** *K1, K2tog* all sts (24 sts)
**Row 87** *K2tog* all sts (12 sts)
**Row 89** *K2tog* all sts (6 sts)
**Row 91** Cast (bind) off.

**EARS** – Make Two Pieces in M and Two Pieces in C
Cast on 10 stitches.
**Row 2** P all evens rows.
**Rows 3-8** Work in St st
**Row 9** K1, SKP, K4, K2tog, K1 (8 sts)
**Row 11** K1, SKP, K2, K2tog, K1 (6 sts)
**Row 13** Cast (bind) off.

**TAIL** - Make One
Cast on 24 stitches in M.
**Row 2** P all even rows.
**Rows 3-6** Work in St st
**Rows 7-10** Change to B and work in St st
**Rows 11-16** Change to M and work in St st
**Rows 17-36** Repeat Rows 7-16 twice more.
**Rows 37-40** Change to B and work in St st

**Row 41** Change to M, working all stitches in it from here. K
**Row 43** *K2, K2tog* all sts (18 sts)
**Row 45** *K1, K2tog* all sts (12 sts)
**Row 47** *K2tog* all sts (6 sts)
Cut the yarn leaving a tail for sewing up. Thread it through the remaining six stitches and pull tightly. Sew up from the thread-through end to the cast on edge using a mattress stitch in M. Leave the cast on edges open.

**FRONT LEGS** - Make Two
Cast on 24 stitches in M.
**Row 2** P all even rows.
**Rows 3-22** Work in St st
**Row 23** *K2, K2tog* all sts (18 sts
**Row 25** *K1, K2tog* all sts (12 sts)
**Row 27** *K2tog* all sts (6 sts)
Cut the yarn leaving a tail for sewing up. Thread it through the remaining six stitches and pull tightly.

**BACK LEGS** - Make Two
Cast on 30 stitches in M.
**Row 2** P all even rows.
**Rows 3-22** Work in St st
**Row 23** *K3, K2tog* all sts (24 sts)
**Row 25** *K2, K2tog* all sts (18 sts)
**Row 27** *K1, K2tog* all sts (12 sts)
**Row 29** *K2tog* all sts (6 sts)
Cut the yarn leaving a tail for sewing up. Thread it through the remaining six stitches and pull tightly.

**NOSE** - Make One
Cast on 3 stitches in B.
**Row 2** P all even rows.
**Row 3** Kfb, Kfb, K1 (5 sts)
**Row 5** K
**Row 7** Cast (bind) off.

**SEWING UP**
Weave in the loose ends. Take the top and under pieces and place the wrong sides together. Sew up using a mattress stitch in M, leaving a hole for stuffing. Stuff the raccoon following the shape of the knit. The neck should have very little stuffing; this allows the face to naturally drop forwards. Once the raccoon is stuffed, it will look like a bowling pin.

Take the toy eyes and place over the colour X scrap yarn markers. Remove the markers and secure with washers. Sew up the hole in the body using a mattress stitch in M. Place the nose in the centre of the snout on the top piece, with the point of the nose just above the cast on edge seam. Sew into place using B.

Take a colour M and colour C ear piece and place the wrong sides together. Sew up using a mattress stitch in C. Leave the cast on edges open and stuff the ear. Repeat for the second ear. Place the first ear between the right-hand set of colour Y scrap yarn markers. Sew the cast on edge of the ear against the knit of the head. Repeat for the second ear, placing it between the left-hand set of colour Y scrap yarn markers and sewing into place. Remove the markers.

Sew up each leg from the thread-through end to cast on edge using a mattress stitch in M. Stuff each leg evenly. Place the back legs 5cm (2in) from the cast (bound) off edge seam, leaving a gap of 9cm (3½in) in the centre between them. They will sit on the sides of the raccoon, facing outwards. Sew the cast on edges of the legs against the knit of the body using M. On each back leg measure 4cm (1½in) from the cast on edge, on the sides facing the tummy. Add a small stitch at this point, sewing from the side of the leg into the body of the raccoon. This will pull the legs in, so they are facing forwards. Place the front legs 13cm (5in) from the cast (bound) off edge seam, leaving a gap of 10cm (4in) in the centre between them. Sew into place using M. Sew the ends of the front legs together using M.

Stuff the tail and place it 3cm (1¼in) from the cast (bound) off edge seam and sew into place using M. Weave in the loose ends.

# CORGI

## MATERIALS

Scheepjes Colour Crafter, 100% acrylic, 300m per 100g (328yd per 3½oz), or any DK yarn

**M** - Gold - 1709 Burum x 1 ball
**C** - White - 1001 Weert x 1 ball
**B** - Black - 1002 Ede x 1 ball
4mm (US 6) straight needles, a handful of toy stuffing, 2 x 10mm toy eyes and washers

## SCRAP YARN MARKERS

Colour **X** – Eye placement
Colour **Y** – Ear placement
Colour **Z** – Leg placement

**TENSION (GAUGE):** 20 sts x 24 rows = 10cm (4in)

**FINISHED SIZE:** 35 x 15 x 10cm (13¾ x 6 x 4in)

**TOP PIECE** – Make One
Cast on 6 stitches in C.
**Row 2** P
**Row 3** *Kfb, K1* all stitches (9 sts)
**Row 4** P
**Rows 5-8** Work in St st
**Row 9** K2M, K5C, K2M
**Row 10** P2M, P5C, P2M
**Rows 11-12** Repeat Rows 9-10
**Row 13** Kfb in M, K1M, K5C, Kfb in M, K1M (11 sts)
**Row 14** P4M, P3C, P4M
**Row 15** K1M, Kfb in M, K1M, Kfb in M, K3C, Kfb in M, K1M, Kfb in M, K1M (15 sts)
**Row 16** P6M, P3C, P6M
**Row 17** K1M, Kfb in M, K2M, Kfb in M, K2M, K1C, K1M, Kfb in M, K2M, Kfb in M, K2M (19 sts)
**Row 18** P9M [add a colour **X** scrap yarn marker to the 6th of these nine stitches], P1C, P9M [add a colour **X** scrap yarn marker to the 4th of these nine stitches]
**Row 19** K9M, K1C, K9M
**Row 20** P9M, P1C, P9M
**Row 21** K8M, K3C, K8M
**Row 22** P8M, P3C, P8M
**Row 23** K7M, K2tog in C, SKP in C, K1M, Kfb in M, K5M (19 sts)
**Row 24** P8M, P4C, P7M
**Row 25** K6M, Kfb in M, SKP in C, K2tog in C, Kfb in M, K7M (19 sts)
**Row 26** P9M [add colour **Y** scrap yarn markers to the 4th and 9th of these nine stitches], P2C, P8M [add colour **Y** scrap yarn markers to the 1st and 6th of these eight stitches].
**Row 27** Work all stitches in M from here. K
**Row 28** P all even rows from here.
**Row 29** K
**Row 31** K4, K3tog, K4, K2tog, K4, K2tog (15 sts)
**Row 33** *K3, K2tog* all stitches (12 sts)
**Row 35** *K2, K2tog* all stitches (9 sts)
**Rows 37-44** Work in St st
**Row 45** K1, Kfb, K4, Kfb, K2 (11 sts)
**Row 47** K
**Row 49** K1, Kfb, K6, Kfb, K2 (13 sts)
**Rows 51-86** Work in St st
**Row 87** K1, SKP, K7, K2tog, K1 (11 sts)
**Row 89** K1, SKP, K5, K2tog, K1 (9 sts)
**Row 91** *K1, K2tog* all stitches (6 sts)
**Row 93** Cast (bind) off.

**UNDER PIECE** – Make One
Cast on 6 stitches in C.
**Row 2** P all even rows until otherwise stated.
**Row 3** *Kfb, K1* all stitches (9 sts)
**Rows 5-14** Work in St st
**Row 15** *Kfb, K2* all stitches (12 sts)
**Row 17** K
**Row 19** *Kfb, K3* all stitches (15 sts)
**Rows 21-30** Work in St st
**Row 31** *Kfb, K4* all stitches (18 sts)

**Row 33** *Kfb, K5* all stitches (21 sts)
**Row 35** K2M, K17C, K2M
**Row 36** P3M, P15C, P3M
**Row 37** Kfb in M, K2M, K4C, Kfb in C, K6C, Kfb in C, K2C, K4M (24 sts)
**Row 38** P4M, P16C, P4M
**Row 39** K4M, K16C, K4M
**Row 40** P4M, P16C, P4M
**Row 41** Kfb in M, K7M, Kfb in C, K7C, Kfb in M, K7M (27 sts)
**Row 42** P9M, P9C [add colour **Z** scrap yarn markers to the 1st and 9th of these nine stitches], P9M
**Row 43** K9M, K9C, K9M
**Row 44** P9M, P9C, P9M
**Row 45** K9M, K9C, K9M
**Row 46** P9M, P9C [add colour **Z** scrap yarn markers to the 1st and 9th of these nine stitches], P9M
**Row 47** K9M, Kfb in C, K2C, Kfb in C, K2C, Kfb in C, K2C, K9M (30 sts)
**Row 48** P9M, P12C, P9M
**Row 49** K9M, Kfb in C, K3C, Kfb in C, K3C, Kfb in C, K3C, K9M (33 sts)
**Row 50** P9M, P15C, P9M
**Row 51** K9M, Kfb in C, K4C, Kfb in C, K4C, Kfb in C, K4C, K9M (36 sts)
**Row 52** P9M, P18C, P9M
**Row 53** K9M, K18C, K9M
**Row 54** P9M, P18C, P9M
**Rows 55-66** Repeat Rows 53-54 six more times.
**Row 67** K9M, K18C, K9M
**Row 68** P9M, P18C [add colour **Z** scrap yarn markers to the 3rd, 8th, 11th and 16th of these

eighteen stitches], P9M

**Row 69** K9M, K18C, K9M

**Row 70** P9M, P18C, P9M

**Rows 71-74** Repeat Rows 69-70 twice more.

**Row 75** K9M, K18C, K9M

**Row 76** P9M, P18C [add colour Z scrap yarn markers to the 3rd, 8th, 11th and 16th of these eighteen stitches], P9M

**Row 77** K9M, K18C, K9M

**Row 78** P9M, P18C, P9M

**Rows 79-80** Repeat Rows 77-78

**Row 81** K10M, K16C, K10M

**Row 82** P12M, P12C, P12M

**Row 83** K4M, K2tog in M, K4M, K2tog in M, K4C, K2tog in C, K4C, K2tog in C, K4M, K2tog in M, K4M, K2tog in M (30 sts)

**Row 84** P11M, P8C, P11M

**Row 85** Work all stitches in M from here. *K3, K2tog* all stitches (24 sts)

**Row 86** P all even rows from here.

**Row 87** *K2, K2tog* all stitches (18 sts)

**Row 89** *K1, K2tog* all stitches (12 sts)

**Row 91** *K2tog* all stitches (6 sts)

**Row 93** Cast (bind) off.

**EARS - Front Piece** - Make Two

Cast on 8 stitches in M.

**Row 2** P

**Row 3** K2M, K4C, K2M

**Row 4** P2M, P4C, P2M

**Rows 5-10** Repeat Rows 3-4 three more times.

**Row 11** K1M, SKP in M, K2C, K2tog in M, K1M (6 sts)

**Row 12** Work all stitches in M from here. P

**Row 13** K1, SKP, K2tog, K1 (4 sts)

**Row 14** P

**Row 15** Cast (bind) off.

**EARS - Back Piece** - Make Two

Cast on 8 stitches in M.

**Row 2** P all even rows.

**Rows 3-10** Work in St st

**Row 11** K1, SKP, K2, K2tog, K1 (6 sts)

**Row 13** K1, SKP, K2tog, K1 (4 sts)

**Row 15** Cast (bind) off.

**LEGS** - Make Four

Cast on 18 stitches in C.

**Row 2** P

**Rows 3-14** Work in St st

**Row 15** *K1, K2tog* all stitches (12 sts)

**Row 16** P

**Row 17** *K2tog* all stitches (6 sts)

Cut the yarn leaving a tail for sewing up, thread it through the remaining six stitches and pull tightly. Sew from the thread-through end to the cast on edge using a mattress stitch. Leave the cast on edge opens.

**TAIL** - Make One

Cast on 18 stitches in M.

**Row 2** P all even rows.

**Rows 3-20** Work in St st

**Row 21** Change to C, working all stitches in it from here. K

**Row 23** K

**Row 25** K

**Row 27** K

**Row 29** *K1, K2tog* all stitches (12 sts)

**Row 31** *K2tog* all stitches (6 sts)

Cut the yarn leaving a tail for sewing up, thread it through the remaining six stitches and pull tightly. Sew from the thread-through end to the cast on edge using a mattress stitch in the corresponding coloured yarn. Leave the cast on edges open.

**NOSE** - Make One

Cast on 4 stitches in B.

**Row 2** P all even rows.

**Row 3** Kfb, K1, Kfb, K1 (6 sts)

**Row 5** K

**Row 7** K1, SKP, K2tog, K1 (4 sts)

**Row 9** Cast (bind) off.

**SEWING UP**

Weave in the loose ends. Take the top and under pieces and place the wrong sides together. Sew up using a mattress stitch in the corresponding coloured yarns, leaving a hole for stuffing. Stuff the corgi following the shape of the knit. Take the 10mm toy eyes and place over the colour X scrap yarn markers. Remove the markers and secure the eyes with washers. Place the nose on the top piece on the centre of the snout, above the cast on edge. Sew into place using B and weave in the loose ends. Sew up the hole in the body using a mattress stitch.

Take a front and back ear piece and place the wrong sides together. Sew up using a mattress stitch in M, leaving the cast on edges open. Add a small amount of stuffing to the ear. Repeat for the second ear. Place the first ear between the right-hand set of colour Y scrap yarn markers. Sew the cast on edges of the ear against the knit of the top piece using M. Place the second ear between the left-hand set of colour Y scrap yarn markers and sew into place.

Stuff the legs evenly. On the under piece of the corgi find the first set of colour Z scrap yarn markers; there will be four of them. Place one front leg between each pair of markers, leaving a gap of 0.5cm (¼in) in the centre between the legs. Sew the cast on edge of the legs against the knit of the body using C.

Find the next set of colour Z scrap yarn markers; there will be eight of them. Place the first of the back legs between the right-hand set of markers and sew into place using C. Repeat for the second back leg, placing it between the left-hand set of markers and sew in place using C.

Stuff the tail evenly. Place it onto the back of the corgi. Sew the tail into the centre of the cast (bound) off edge seam using M. Remove all markers and weave in the loose ends.

# STARFISH

**MATERIALS**

Scheepjes Colour Crafter, 100% acrylic, 300m per 100g (328yd per 3½oz), or any DK yarn
**M** – Copper – 1711 Leeuwarden x 1 ball
**C** – Gold – 1709 Burum x 1 ball
4mm (US 6) straight needles,
stitch holder, a handful of toy stuffing,

2 x 10mm toy eyes and washers, black DK yarn for embroidery

**TENSION (GAUGE):** 20 sts x 24 rows = 10cm (4in)

**FINISHED SIZE:** 18 x 18 x 2cm (7 x 7 x ¾in)

**TOP PIECE** – Make One
Cast on 5 stitches in M.
**Row 2** P all even rows.
**Row 3** *Kfb* all stitches (10 sts)
**Row 5** *Kfb* all stitches (20 sts)
**Row 7** *Kfb, P1* all stitches (30 sts)
**Row 9** *Kfb, P2* all stitches (40 sts)
**Row 11** *Kfb, P3* all stitches (50 sts)

*Leg One*
**Row 13** K1, P4, Kfb, P3, K1
(11 sts), TURN, placing the remaining 40 stitches on a holder to be worked later.
**Row 15** K1, P4, K1, P4, K1
**Row 17** K1, P4, K1, P4, K1
**Row 19** K1, P2tog, P2, K1, P2, P2tog, K1 (9 sts)
**Row 21** K1, P3, K1, P3, K1
**Row 23** K1, P3, K1, P3, K1
**Row 25** K1, P3, K1, P3, K1
**Row 27** K1, P2tog, P1, K1, P1, P2tog, K1 (7 sts)
**Row 29** K1, P2, K1, P2, K1
**Row 31** K1, P2tog, K1, P2tog, K1 (5 sts)
**Row 33** K1, K3tog, K1 (3 sts)
**Row 35** Cast (bind) off.

*Leg Two*
Move 10 stitches from the holder onto the left-hand needle ready to be worked from Row 13. Leave the remaining 30 stitches on the holder to be worked later.
**Rows 13** Reattach the yarn and K1, P4, Kfb, P3, K1

**Rows 14-35** Repeat the instructions for leg one.

*Legs Three, Four and Five*
Repeat the instructions for leg two.

**UNDER PIECE** – Make One
Cast on 5 stitches in C.
**Row 2** P all even rows.
**Row 3** *Kfb* all stitches (10 sts)
**Row 5** *Kfb* all stitches (20 sts)
**Row 7** *Kfb, K1* all stitches (30 sts)
**Row 9** *Kfb, K2* all stitches (40 sts)
**Row 11** *Kfb, K3* all stitches (50 sts)

*Leg One*
**Row 13** K5, Kfb, K4 (11 sts), TURN, placing the remaining 40 stitches on a holder to be worked later.
**Row 15** K5, B1, K5 [B refers to the bobble stitch; see page 5]
**Row 17** K
**Row 19** K1, SKP, K2, B1, K2, K2tog, K1 (9 sts)
**Row 21** K
**Row 23** K4, B1, K4
**Row 25** K
**Row 27** K1, SKP, K1, B1, K1, K2tog, K1 (7 sts)
**Row 29** K
**Row 31** K1, SKP, B1, K2tog, K1 (5 sts)
**Row 33** K1, K3tog, K1 (3 sts)
**Row 35** Cast (bind) off.

*Leg Two*
Move 10 stitches from the holder onto the left-hand needle ready

to be worked from Row 13. Leave the remaining 30 stitches on the holder to be worked later.
**Rows 13** Reattach the yarn and K5, Kfb, K4
**Rows 14-35** Repeat the instructions for leg one.

*Legs Three, Four and Five*
Repeat the instructions for leg two.

**SEWING UP**
Weave in the loose ends. On the top piece of the starfish, sew up the gap from the cast on edge to the turn of the legs using a mattress stitch in M. Repeat for the under piece of the starfish, sewing up in C. Take the top and under pieces and place the wrong sides together. Sew up using a mattress stitch in M. Stuff each leg as you go, following the shape of the knit, and leave a small hole for adding the eyes.

With the top of the starfish facing towards you, place the 10mm eyes in the centre of the face, leaving a gap of 2cm (¾in) between them. Secure in place with washers. Embroider a small smile 1cm (⅜in) under the eyes using the black DK yarn. Add any additional stuffing if needed and sew up the hole in the body using a mattress stitch in M. Weave in the loose ends.

# KNITTER'S BINGO

WHEN YOU'RE IN THE WILD KNITTING, LISTEN OUT FOR THESE QUESTIONS AND PHRASES. A FULL HOUSE MAKES YOU THE KNITTIEST KNITTER OF ALL TIME.

| | | | | |
|---|---|---|---|---|
| Me mam used to do that. | Can you make me one of those? | I tried knitting once but it was too hard. | Did you make that? (when wearing anything knitted) | I crochet, therefore I can't knit. |
| What yarn is that? | You should start your own business selling those. | You must be really patient! | How can you do that without looking? | What are you making? |
| Can you teach me to knit? | Knit one, purl one. | FREE SPACE | Who taught you to knit? | I find wool too itchy. |
| Why don't you stop knitting, just for one night? | Where did you get that (hand knitted item) from? | Can I pay you to knit something for me? | Are you allowed to bring needles on the plane? | My nan is an amazing knitter! |
| Can you knit something for my dog? | Want to come to knit and natter at the pub? | Isn't acrylic yarn really squeaky and horrible? | How long will that take? | You don't see many people knitting anymore. |

One of these balls is from a different dye lot. It is a slightly different shade. Can you spot which one is it?

ANSWER ON PAGE 110

# Swan Door Stop

Welcome to a secret instalment of the Curious Project. Did you guess what it could have been? In July 2017 we launched a monthly mystery knitting kit where curious knitters would be given a clue at the beginning of the month and a few weeks later would receive a kit based on that clue. This project was originally intended for one of our first six bags, but we decided it wasn't quite right. It didn't fit with the second or third set of bags either, so the swan was pushed to the back of the SL vaults. After collecting dust for over a year, we're excited to finally release it into the wild as part of this very special Curious Project.

Sincerely Louise

## Materials
Cygnet Seriously Chunky, 100% acrylic, 48m per 100g (52yd per 3½oz) , or any chunky (bulky) yarn
**A** – Gold (metallic) x 20g (¾oz)
**B** – Black x 20g (¾oz)
**C** – Cream x 4 balls
9mm (US 13) straight needles, 150g (5oz) toy stuffing, 2 x 20mm toy eyes and washers

## Scrap Yarn Markers
Colour X - Eye placement
Colour Y - Neck placement

**You will also need:** 1kg (2lb) of sand poured into an old pair of tights and tied securely

**Tension (Gauge):** 8 sts x 11 rows = 10cm (4in)
**Finished Size:** 80 x 38 x 18cm (31½ x 15 x 7in)

**TOP PIECE** – Make One
Cast on 3 stitches in A.
**Row 2** P all even rows.
**Row 3** *Kfb* all stitches (6 sts)
**Rows 5-10** Work in St st
**Row 11** Change to B, working all stitches in it until stated. K
**Row 13** *Kfb, K1* all stitches (9 sts)
**Row 15** Change to C, working all stitches in it from here. K
**Row 17** Kfb, K2 [add a colour X scrap yarn marker to the 1st of these two stitches], Kfb, K2 [add a colour X scrap yarn marker to the 2nd of these two stitches], Kfb, K2 (12 sts)
**Row 19** *Kfb, K3* all stitches (15 sts)
**Row 21** K
**Row 23** K
**Row 25** *K3, K2tog* all sts (12 sts)
**Row 27** *K2, K2tog* all sts (9 sts)
**Row 29** *K1, K2tog* all sts (6 sts)
**Rows 31-48** Work in St st
**Row 49** K [add a colour Y scrap yarn marker to the 3rd of these sts]
**Rows 51-60** Work in St st
**Row 61** *Kfb, K1* all stitches (9 sts)
**Row 63** *Kfb, K2* all stitches (12 sts)
**Row 65** K [add a colour Y scrap yarn marker to the 6th of these sts]
**Rows 67-90** Work in St st
**Row 91** K1, SKP, K6, K2tog, K1 (10 sts)
**Row 93** K1, SKP, K4, K2tog, K1 (8 sts)
**Row 95** K1, SKP, K2, K2tog, K1 (6 sts)
**Row 97** K1, SKP, K2tog, K1 (4 sts)
**Row 99** Cast (bind) off.

**UNDER PIECE** – Make One
Cast on 3 stitches in A.
**Row 2** P all even rows.
**Row 3** *Kfb* all stitches (6 sts)
**Row 5** K
**Row 7** K
**Row 9** K
**Row 11** Change to C, working all stitches in it from here. K
**Row 13** K
**Row 15** *Kfb, K1* all stitches (9 sts)
**Row 17** K
**Row 19** K
**Row 21** K [add a colour Y scrap yarn marker to the 5th of these sts]
**Row 23** K
**Row 25** *Kfb, K2* all stitches (12 sts)
**Row 27** K [add a colour Y scrap yarn marker to the 6th of these sts]
**Rows 29-50** Work in St st
**Row 51** *Kfb, K3* all stitches (15 sts)

**Row 53** *Kfb, K4* all stitches (18 sts)
**Row 55** *Kfb, K5* all stitches (21 sts)
**Row 57** *Kfb, K6* all stitches (24 sts)
**Row 59** *Kfb, K7* all stitches (27 sts)
**Row 61** *Kfb, K8* all stitches (30 sts)
**Rows 63-88** Work in St st
**Row 89** *K3, K2tog* all stitches (24 sts)
**Row 91** *K2, K2tog* all stitches (18 sts)
**Row 93** *K1, K2tog* all stitches (12 sts)
**Row 95** *K2tog* all stitches (6 sts)
**Row 97** K1, SKP, K2tog, K1 (4 sts)
**Row 99** Cast (bind) off.

**WING - Left Side** – Make One
Cast on 6 stitches in C.
**Row 2** P
**Row 3** *Kfb* all stitches (12 sts)
**Row 4** P1, K1, P2, K1, P2, K1, P2, K1, P1
**Row 5** Kfb, P1, K2, P1, K2, P1, K2, P1, Kfb (14 sts)
**Row 6** *P2, K1* four times, P2
**Row 7** *K2, P1* four times, K2
**Row 8** *P2, K1* four times, P2
**Row 9** *K2, P1* four times, Kfb, K1 (15 sts)
**Row 10** P3, *K1, P2* four times
**Row 11** *K2, P1* four times, K1, Kfb, K1 (16 sts)
**Row 12** P4, *K1, P2* four times
**Row 13** *K2, P1* four times, K2, Kfb, K1 (17 sts)
**Row 14** P5, *K1, P2* four times
**Row 15** *K2, P1* four times, K5
**Row 16** P5, *K1, P2* four times
**Row 17** *K2, P1* four times, K2, K2tog, K1 (16 sts)
**Row 18** P4, *K1, P2* four times
**Row 19** *K2, P1* four times, K1, K2tog, K1 (15 sts)
**Row 20** P3, *K1, P2* four times
**Row 21** K1, SKP, *K2, P1* three times, K2tog, K1 (13 sts)
**Row 22** *P2, K1* three times, P4
**Row 23** K1, SKP, K1, P1, K2, P1, K2, K2tog, K1 (11 sts)
**Row 24** P4, K1, P2, K1, P3
**Row 25** K1, SKP, P1, SKP, P1, K1, K2tog, K1 (8 sts)
**Row 26** P3, K1, P1, K1, P2
**Row 27** K1, SKP, SKP, K2tog, K1 (5 sts)
**Row 28** P
**Row 29** Cast (bind) off.

**WING - Right Side** – Make One
Cast on 6 stitches in C.
**Row 2** P
**Row 3** *Kfb* all stitches (12 sts)
**Row 4** P1, K1, P2, K1, P2, K1, P2, K1, P1
**Row 5** Kfb, P1, K2, P1, K2, P1, K2, P1, Kfb (14 sts)
**Row 6** *P2, K1* four times, P2
**Row 7** *K2, P1* four times, K2
**Row 8** *P2, K1* four times, P2
**Row 9** Kfb, K1, *P1, K2* four times (15 sts)
**Row 10** *P2, K1* four times, P3
**Row 11** Kfb, K2, *P1, K2* four times (16 sts)
**Row 12** *P2, K1* four times, P4
**Row 13** Kfb, K3, *P1, K2* four times (17 sts)
**Row 14** *P2, K1* four times, P5
**Row 15** K5, *P1, K2* four times
**Row 16** *P2, K1* four times, P5
**Row 17** K1, SKP, K2, *P1, K2* four times (16 sts)
**Row 18** *P2, K1* four times, P4
**Row 19** K1, SKP, K1, *P1, K2* four times (15 sts)
**Row 20** *P2, K1* four times, K3
**Row 21** K1, SKP, *P1, K2* three times, K2tog, K1 (13 sts)
**Row 22** P4, *K1, P2* three times
**Row 23** K1, SKP, K2, P1, K2, P1, K1, K2tog, K1 (11 sts)
**Row 24** P3, K1, P2, K1, P4
**Row 25** K1, SKP, K1, P1, K2tog, P1, K2tog, K1 (8 sts)
**Row 26** P2, K1, P1, K1, P3
**Row 27** K1, SKP, K2tog, K2tog, K1 (5 sts)
**Row 28** P
**Row 29** Cast (bind) off.

# Sewing up

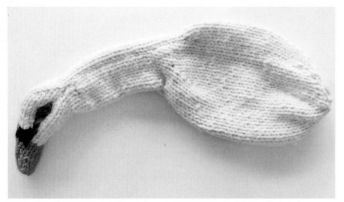

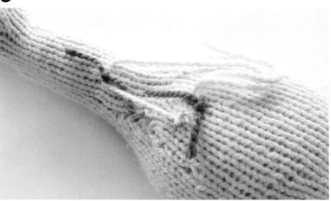

**1.** Take the top and under pieces and place the wrong sides together. Sew up using a mattress stitch in C. Leave a hole in the top of the head and body. Place the sand-filled tights into the body of the swan and then stuff, following the shape of the knit. Place the eyes over the colour X markers and secure with the washers. Remove the markers and sew up the hole in the body.

**2.** Lay the swan flat so the top piece is facing towards you. There will be two colour Y scrap yarn markers on the top piece, in the centre of the neck with several rows between them. Using some C yarn, sew into where one of the markers is. Secure the yarn by sewing several times into the top piece. Sew from the first marker to the second, then sew back into the first marker.

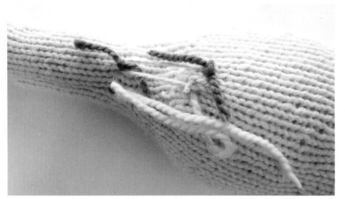

**3.** Repeat this process several times, sewing between the two markers.

**4.** Pull the yarn as you sew up. This will pull the stitches together and raise the neck backwards.

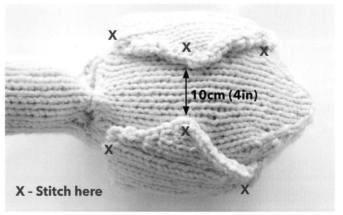

**5.** Find the two colour Y scrap yarn markers on the under piece, in the centre of the neck with several rows between them. Repeat steps 2–4 to pull the underside of the neck together, giving the swan its shape. Remove all the markers and weave in the loose ends.

**6.** Place the wings on the top piece, with the cast on edge in line with the pulled stitch and the cast (bound) off edge 11cm (4¼in) from the cast (bound) off edge of the body. Leave a gap of 10cm (4in) between them. Sew the cast on edge in place using C and add two stitches at the top of the wing and at the cast (bound) off edge.

# THE Knitter's Arms

# PUB QUIZ

# PUB QUIZ

## THE RULES
The quiz has six rounds: a picture round, general knit knowledge, who's the designer, film and TV, music, and celebrity knitters. Each round states how many points you'll receive per correct answer. Play with your knitting friends or quiz yourself!

Team Name: ..........................................................................................

## ROUND ONE - PICTURE ROUND
Name the knit stitch. 1 point per correct answer                    Total:        /9

..................................................

..................................................

..................................................

..................................................

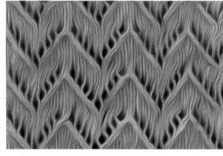

..................................................

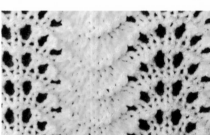

..................................................

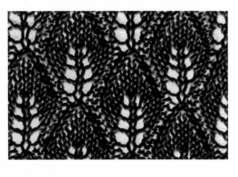

..................................................

..................................................

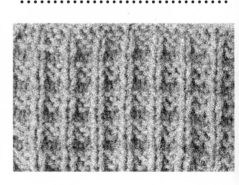

..................................................

## ROUND TWO – GENERAL KNIT KNOWLEDGE
1 point per correct answer                           Total:    /10

**1.** What is the name of the four needles used to work in the round?

**2.** St st is an abbreviation for what?

**3.** A UK size 8 (US 6) needle is the equivalent to which metric size?

**4.** What does knitflix mean?

**5.** The name of which yarn weight derives from a Norfolk village?

**6.** In 2012 where did knitters meet to break a world record?

**7.** What ailment do knitters face when making more than one thing?

**8.** What is the term for tiny crocheted or knitted toys?

**9.** Which island is situated between Orkney and Shetland?

**10.** How many calories do you burn when knitting for half an hour?

## ROUND THREE – WHO'S THE DESIGNER
1 point per correct answer                           Total:    /10

**1.** Shawl king

**2.** Known for her tiny birds and toys

**3.** Brand behind Spike the Tinsel Hedgehog

**4.** Blanket designer inspired by tiles

**5.** Colourful knitwear designer who works with Rowan

**6.** Crocheter of an animal menagerie

**7.** *Woodland Knits* author known for her hexipuff blanket

**8.** Fabulous sock knitter, yeah!

**9.** Classic British designer, as seen in John Lewis

**10.** Sophie's Universe designer

## ROUND FOUR - FILM AND TV
1 point per correct answer

Total:    /10

**1.** Which product featured the strap line 'knitted by nanas'?

**2.** Which kids TV show was full of noisy pink characters?

**3.** Who had a hand knitted jumper with the letter 'R' delivered to him?

**4.** Which famous doctor wears a colourful scarf?

**5.** Which TV show features the Old Muddy River Bridge Knitathon?

**6.** Which animated animal can often be found knitting?

**7.** When she's not knitting, she's solving crimes. Who is she?

**8.** What 2014 film features a vampire called Deacon who loves to knit?

**9.** Which 2018 film featured a shawl that was loved so much the costume designer published the pattern for free?

**10.** 'The One With The Red Sweater' was an episode of which TV show?

## ROUND FIVE - MUSIC
Name the band and song; each has a link to craft.
1 point per correct band and 1 point per correct song

Total:    /20

**1.** Dancing in the disco, bumper to bumper

**2.** You've got to pick up every stitch

**3.** I'm knitting jumpers, I'm working after hours

**4.** Those blackbirds look like knitting needles, trying to peck your head

**5.** You spin me right round

**6.** If I could've held you, I would've held you

**7.** My heart comes undone, slowly unravels in a ball of yarn

**8.** I said maybe, you're gonna be the one that saves me

**9.** Would you be a happy boy or a girl, if I could I would give you the world

**10.** I'm knitting with only one needle, unravelling fast it's true

## ROUND SIX - CELEBRITY KNITTERS

Name the celebrity knitters who appear in these films and TV shows. You'll receive 1 point per correct answer. Get all 10 correct and your score is doubled to 20 points. But get any incorrect and you score 0 in this round, so it might be safer to leave answers blank if you're unsure.

Total: /20

**1.** *The Notebook*

**2.** *Jessica Jones*

**3.** *Notting Hill*

**4.** *Grumpy Old Women*

**5.** *Sex in the City*

**6.** *Pulp Fiction*

**7.** *Les Misérables* (film)

**8.** *The Darling Buds of May*

**9.** *My Fair Lady*

**10.** *Mad Men*

## BONUS QUESTIONS

Total: /15

**1.** What year was the first knitting machine made?
   5 points for the correct answer, 2 points for within 10 years

**2.** Name eight yarn weights.
   1 point for each correct answer

**3.** How many officially recognized alpaca shades are there?
   2 points for the correct answer

THE
**Knitter's Arms**

THANKS
FOR PLAYING

## FIND THE ANSWERS ON PAGE 108

| | |
|---|---|
| **1.** Picture Round | /9 |
| **2.** General Knit Knowledge | /10 |
| **3.** Who's the Designer | /10 |
| **4.** Film and TV | /10 |
| **5.** Music | /20 |
| **6.** Celebrity Knitters | /20 |
| **7.** Bonus Questions | /15 |
| **FINAL SCORE** | **/94** |

# GIANT BALLOON DOG

**MATERIALS**

Sincerely Louise Mythically Chunky,
100% acrylic, 48m per 100g (52yd per 3½oz),
or any chunky (bulky) yarn
**M** – Blue – Mermaid x 22 balls

9mm (US 13) straight needles, row counter,
4kg (9lb) toy stuffing
**TENSION (GAUGE):** 8 sts x 11 rows = 10cm (4in)
**FINISHED SIZE:** 120 x 110 x 20cm (47 x 43 x 8in)

The balloon dog is worked in one piece, starting with the tail. Use a row counter when knitting. After each section of the project, reset the row counter. You don't need to cast (bind) off and cast on again. Just reset the row counter and continue as usual. Try making a smaller version using DK yarn and the appropriate sized knitting needles.

**TAIL**

Cast on 6 stitches in M.
**Row 2** P all even rows unless otherwise stated. P rows have been <u>underlined</u>.
**Row 3** *Kfb* all stitches (12 sts)
**Rows 5-14** Work in St st
**Row 15** *Kfb* all stitches (24 sts)
**Row 17** *Kfb, K1* all stitches (36 sts)
**Row 19** *Kfb, K2* all stitches (48 sts)
**Rows 21-48** Work in St st
**Row 49** *K2, K2tog* all stitches (36 sts)
**Row 51** *K1, K2tog* all stitches (24 sts)
**Row 53** *K2tog* all stitches (12 sts)

**Row 55** *K2tog* all stitches (6 sts)
<u>**Row 56** P</u>

**1ST BACK LEG**

**Row 1** *Kfb* all stitches (12 sts)
**Row 3** *Kfb* all stitches (24 sts)
**Row 5** *Kfb, K1* all stitches (36 sts)
**Row 7** *Kfb, K2* all stitches (48 sts)
**Rows 9-64** Work in St st
**Row 65** *K2, K2tog* all stitches (36 sts)
**Row 67** *K1, K2tog* all stitches (24 sts)
**Row 69** *K2tog* all stitches (12 sts)
**Row 71** *K2tog* all stitches (6 sts)
<u>**Row 72** P</u>

**2ND BACK LEG**

Repeat the instructions for the 1st back leg.

**BODY**

**Row 1** *Kfb* all stitches (12 sts)
**Row 3** *Kfb* all stitches (24 sts)
**Row 5** *Kfb, K1* all stitches (36 sts)
**Row 7** *Kfb, K2* all stitches (48 sts)
**Rows 9-44** Work in St st
**Row 45** *K2, K2tog* all stitches (36 sts)

**Row 47** *K1, K2tog* all stitches (24 sts)
**Row 49** *K2tog* all stitches (12 sts)
**Row 51** *K2tog* all stitches (6 sts)
<u>**Row 52** P</u>

**1ST FRONT LEG**

Repeat the instructions for the 1st back leg.

**2ND FRONT LEG**

Repeat the instructions for the 1st back leg.

**NECK**

**Row 1** *Kfb* all stitches (12 sts)
**Row 3** *Kfb* all stitches (24 sts)
**Row 5** *Kfb, K1* all stitches (36 sts)
**Row 7** *Kfb, K2* all stitches (48 sts)
**Rows 9-32** Work in St st
**Row 33** *K2, K2tog* all stitches (36 sts)
**Row 35** *K1, K2tog* all stitches (24 sts)
**Row 37** *K2tog* all stitches (12 sts)
**Row 39** *K2tog* all stitches (6 sts)
<u>**Row 40** P</u>

## 1ST EAR

**Row 1** *Kfb* all stitches (12 sts)
**Row 3** *Kfb* all stitches (24 sts)
**Row 5** *Kfb, K1* all stitches (36 sts)
**Row 7** *Kfb, K2* all stitches (48 sts)
**Rows 9-40** Work in St st
**Row 41** *K2, K2tog* all stitches (36 sts)
**Row 43** *K1, K2tog* all stitches (24 sts)
**Row 45** *K2tog* all stitches (12 sts)
**Row 47** *K2tog* all stitches (6 sts)
**Row 48** P

## 2ND EAR

Repeat the instructions for the 1st ear.

## FACE

**Row 1** *Kfb* all stitches (12 sts)
**Row 3** *Kfb* all stitches (24 sts)
**Row 5** *Kfb, K1* all stitches (36 sts)
**Row 7** *Kfb, K2* all stitches (48 sts)
**Rows 9-38** Work in St st
**Row 39** *K2, K2tog* all sts (36 sts)

**Row 41** *K1, K2tog* all sts (24 sts)
**Row 43** *K2tog* all stitches (12 sts)
**Row 45** K
**Row 47** K
**Row 49** *Kfb* all stitches (24 sts)
**Row 51** *Kfbf* all stitches (72 sts)
**Row 53** Cast (bind) off.

# SEWING UP

You can also watch our short video on how to sew up your dog here: www.sincerelylouise.co.uk/balloondog

**1.** Take the dog and sew up each section using a mattress stitch in M. Leave a hole in each section for stuffing. Stuff each section evenly and sew up the holes using a mattress stitch in M. Lay the dog flat across the floor in front of you with the tail on the right-hand side, ready to be put together.

**2.** Place the first and second back legs so they are facing towards you. Wrap the thin piece connecting the second leg and body around the thin piece connecting the first leg and tail. Twist both legs around. Repeat the twist again and sew several stitches in M around the thin pieces of the knit to secure.

**3.** Lay the body section flat. Place the front two legs so they are facing towards you. Twist the thin piece connecting the second leg and the neck around the thin piece connecting the first leg and body. Twist both legs around. Repeat the twist again and sew several stitches around the thin pieces to secure.

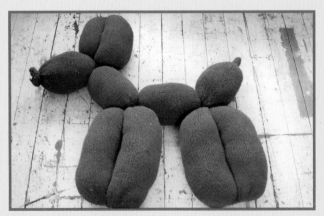

**4.** Place the neck so it is facing north-west. Twist the second ear piece connecting to the nose around the thin piece connecting the first ear and neck. Twist both ears around. Repeat the twist again and sew several stitches in M around the thin pieces of the knit to secure. Weave in all the loose ends.

Sincerely Louise starts life as an Instagram account whilst I study photography at the Arts University Bournemouth.

In January my Woolly Heads are discovered and suddenly go viral. I even make an appearance on *The Alan Titchmarsh Show*.

F+W media commissions me to write a book. I spend the winter designing the patterns. I move to North London.

I suffer huge blood clots in both my lungs and take some time off work.

I become obsessed with knitting and start making props for my photo projects.

Following the Boden launch, *Tatler* features my work in their magazine. I start selling ready-made animal heads at Molly Meg, a children's boutique.

I exhibit at my first fair, the Knitting & Stitching Show at Ally Pally, and almost sell out of books on the first day. After the show I start listing more items on Etsy.

## 2011    2012    2013    2014    2015

I learn to knit and start making fox scarves. I sell a few finished pieces on Etsy whilst studying. I haven't discovered Ravelry yet, so make up the patterns myself. The knits are a little crude, but I'm proud of them.

I graduate and move back to Essex, spending the rest of the year knitting. I take on a part-time job with an independent knitting designer in London and begin selling her products at Covent Garden Market.

Knit Today and Crafty magazines commission me to write fox-themed knitting patterns. Both are my first attempts at pattern writing and both make the cover.

In September Faux Taxidermy Knits is released and Sincerely Louise is officially born. I launch my first four animal head kits at the Farnham Maltings shop.

I make a series of fashion images called Woolly Heads, which feature women in knitted wigs, as part of my final major project at university.

I'm approached by Boden who commission me to make six faux taxidermy animal heads for their press launch at Somerset House.

The publishers come back with the photos for the book, but I end up reshooting them myself. Doing all this almost takes me out of business. I move to South London.

After spending the summer recovering I decide to take a small studio space at Eurolink Business Centre in Brixton.

# History of Sincerely Louise

I'm asked to exhibit at the Clothes Show Live, teaching the public how to knit with a small army of knitters.

Myself and my friend Bex start putting on knitting nights at my studio in Brixton.

Sincerely Louise collaborates with Cygnet Yarns on a range of wool called Mythically Chunky.

I'm granted a start-up loan and start investing in new product lines and take on my first two assistants.

I start a project called the Scrap Yarn Challenge, asking the audience what some of my stash should be knitted into.

I'm asked to speak about crafts on *Woman's Hour* on BBC Radio 4.

Sincerely Louise launches its first range of yarn and a jumper pattern collection under the name How Does It Feel?

I take a trip to India and the team exhibit at Unravel without me and have a fabulous time.

Eurolink decides to almost double our studio rent. My partner and myself decide to finally leave London and move to Sheffield, finding a new space in an old cutlery factory.

## 2016    2017    2018

I write some patterns for the Mollie Makes: How to Knit book that are featured on the cover.

I enter the Etsy Awards and am somehow successful with my application. I go on to win the People's Choice Award – the grand prize.

I host my first event, the Mythical Winter party in Waterloo, as a thank you to everyone who voted in the Etsy Awards.

Octavia joins Sincerely Louise as a graphic designer. She gets to work on designing the clues for the Curious Project, our mystery knitting kit, that launches in July.

We start work on this book.

Eleanor joins the SL team as our new studio assistant. I'm asked to collaborate with the V&A on a special mini faux taxidermy workshop.

I sadly say goodbye to the team and head up north for a new chapter of Sincerely Louise.

# PRETTY PLATYPUS SCARF

## MATERIALS

Rico Fashion Metallise Aran, 58% polyester, 42% wool, 145m per 50g (158yd per 1¾oz), or any Aran (worsted) yarn
**M** - Powder x 4 balls

Stylecraft Life Chunky, 25% wool, 75% acrylic, 148m per 100g (162yd per 3½oz), or any chunky (bulky) yarn
**C** - Cream x 1 ball

5mm (US 8) straight needles (you can use DPNs from Row 213), 2 x 20mm toy eyes and washers

### Scrap Yarn Markers
Colour X - Eye placement
Colour Y - Folding and sewing

### Tension (Gauge):
**M** - 20 sts x 26 rows = 10cm (4in)
**C** - 16 sts x 22 rows = 10cm (4in)
**Finished Size:** 14 x 200cm (5½ x 79in)

The best way to work the scarf is by knitting the tail first; this way you won't run out of yarn for the body. Take the Rico yarn from the middle of the ball as it can tangle easily. Use the same needles for both yarns; the tension will be slightly different.

**TAIL** - Make One
Cast on 48 stitches in M.
**Row 2** P all even rows.
**Rows 3-10** Work in St st
**Row 11** *Kfb, K7* all stitches (54 sts)
**Rows 13-20** Work in St st
**Row 21** *Kfb, K8* all stitches (60 sts)
**Rows 23-36** Work in St st
**Row 37** *K8, K2tog* all stitches (54 sts)
**Rows 39-48** Work in St st
**Row 49** *K7, K2tog* all stitches (48 sts)
**Rows 51-56** Work in St st
**Row 57** *K6, K2tog* all stitches (42 sts)
**Row 59** K
**Row 61** *K5, K2tog* all stitches (36 sts)
**Row 63** *K4, K2tog* all stitches (30 sts)
**Row 65** *K3, K2tog* all stitches (24 sts)
**Row 67** *K2, K2tog* all stitches (18 sts)
**Row 69** *K1, K2tog* all stitches (12 sts)
**Row 71** Cast (bind) off.

**SCARF** - Make One
Cast on 2 stitches in M.
**Row 2** P all even rows.
**Row 3** Kfb, Kfb (4 sts)
**Row 5** Kfb, K1, Kfb, K1 (6 sts)
**Row 7** Kfb, K3, Kfb, K1 (8 sts)
**Row 9** Kfb, K5, Kfb, K1 (10 sts)
**Row 11** Kfb, K7, Kfb, K1 (12 sts)
**Row 13** Kfb, K9, Kfb, K1 (14 sts)
**Row 15** Kfb, K11, Kfb, K1 (16 sts)
**Row 17** Kfb, K13, Kfb, K1 (18 sts)
**Row 19** Kfb, K15, Kfb, K1 (20 sts)
**Row 21** Kfb, K17, Kfb, K1 (22 sts)
**Row 23** Kfb, K19, Kfb, K1 (24 sts)
**Row 25** Kfb, K21, Kfb, K1 (26 sts)
**Row 27** Kfb, K23, Kfb, K1 (28 sts)
**Rows 29-34** Work in St st
**Row 35** K1, SKP, K22, K2tog, K1 (26 sts)
**Rows 37-40** Work in St st
**Row 41** Kfb, K23, Kfb, K1 (28 sts)
**Row 43** K
**Row 45** Kfb, K25, Kfb, K1 (30 sts)
**Rows 47-58** Work in St st
**Row 59** K1, SKP, K24, K2tog, K1 (28 sts)
**Row 61** K
**Row 63** K1, SKP, K22, K2tog, K1 (26 sts)
**Row 65** K

**Row 137** Kfb, K15, Kfb, K1 (20 sts)
**Row 139** Change to M, working all stitches in it from here. Kfb, K17, Kfb, K1 (22 sts)
**Row 141** Kfb, K19, Kfb, K1 (24 sts)
**Row 143** Kfb, K21, Kfb, K1 (26 sts)
**Row 145** K [add colour X scrap yarn markers to the 5th and 22nd of these stitches]
**Row 147** Kfb, K23, Kfb, K1 (28 sts)
**Row 149** K
**Row 151** Kfb, K25, Kfb, K1 (30 sts)
**Rows 153-164** Work in St st
**Row 165** K1, SKP, K24, K2tog, K1 (28 sts)
**Row 167** K
**Row 169** K1, SKP, K22, K2tog, K1 (26 sts)
**Rows 171-174** Work in St st
**Row 175** Kfb, K23, Kfb, K1 (28 sts)
**Rows 177-182** Work in St st
**Row 183** Kfb, K25, Kfb, K1 (30 sts)
**Row 185** Kfb, K27, Kfb, K1 (32 sts)
**Row 187** Kfb, K29, Kfb, K1 (34 sts)
**Row 189** Kfb, K31, Kfb, K1 (36 sts)
**Row 191** Kfb, K33, Kfb, K1 (38 sts)
**Row 193** Kfb, K35, Kfb, K1 (40 sts)
**Row 195** Kfb, K37, Kfb, K1 (42 sts)
**Row 197** Kfb, K39, Kfb, K1 (44 sts)
**Row 199** Kfb, K41, Kfb, K1 (46 sts)
**Row 201** Kfb, K43, Kfb, K1 (48 sts)
**Row 203** Kfb, K45, Kfb, K1 (50 sts
**Row 205** Kfb, K47, Kfb, K1 (52 sts)
**Row 207** Kfb, K49, Kfb, K1 (54 sts)
**Row 209** Kfb, K51, Kfb, K1 (56 sts)
**Row 211** K [add colour Y scrap yarn markers to the first and last sts].
Work in St st until the piece measures approximately 180cm (71in) from the colour Y markers placed at Row 105. It is important to make sure there is yarn remaining to cast (bind) off and sew the scarf up.
Note that from **Row 213** you can either continue to work the piece flat in St st (knit one row, purl one row) or you can join the work and use DPNs, or a short pair of circular needles, and knit every row in the round.

**FEET** - Make Four
Cast on 6 stitches in C.
**Row 2** K all even rows.
**Row 3** *Kfb, K1* all stitches (9 sts)
**Row 5** K
**Row 7** K
**Row 9** *Kfb, K2* all stitches (12 sts)
**Row 11** K
**Row 13** K

*End of the Foot – Spike One*
**Row 15** K3, TURN, placing the remaining 9 stitches on a holder to be worked later.
**Row 16** K the three stitches.
**Row 17** K
**Row 19** K3tog (1 st)
Cut the yarn leaving a small tail. Thread it through the remaining stitch and pull tightly. Weave in the loose end.

*End of the Foot – Spike Two*
Move three stitches from the holder onto the left-hand needle ready to be worked from Row 15.
**Row 15** Reattach the yarn and K
**Row 17** K
**Row 19** K3tog (1 st)
Cut the yarn leaving a small tail. Thread it through the remaining stitch and pull tightly. Weave in the loose end.

*End of the Foot – Spikes Three and Four*
Repeat the instructions for spike two.

**SEWING UP**
Weave in the loose ends. If your scarf has been knitted flat, sew up the body to the colour Y scrap yarn markers placed at Row 211 using a mattress stitch in M. Fold the bill of the platypus at the colour Y scrap yarn markers placed at Row 105. The cast on edge will meet the colour Y scrap yarn markers at Row 211. Sew up using a mattress stitch in the corresponding coloured yarns, leaving a hole.

Place the 20mm eyes over the colour X scrap yarn markers. Secure with washers, remove all markers and sew up the hole in the scarf. Place two of the feet 33cm (13in) from where the scarf was folded at Row 105, one on either side of the scarf, and sew into place using C. Place the tail in the centre of the bottom of the scarf and sew into place using M. Place the other two feet either side of the tail and sew into place using C. Weave in the loose ends.

**Row 67** K1, SKP, K20, K2tog, K1 (24 sts)
**Row 69** K1, SKP, K18, K2tog, K1 (22 sts)
**Row 71** K1, SKP, K16, K2tog, K1 (20 sts)
**Row 73** Change to C, working all stitches in it from here. K1, SKP, K14, K2tog, K1 (18 sts)
**Rows 75-78** Work in St st
**Row 79** Kfb, K15, Kfb, K1 (20 sts)
**Rows 81-84** Work in St st
**Row 85** Kfb, K17, Kfb, K1 (22 sts)
**Rows 87-94** Work in St st
**Row 95** Kfb, K19, Kfb, K1 (24 sts)
**Row 97** K
**Row 99** *K2, K2tog* all stitches (18 sts)
**Row 101** *K1, K2tog* all stitches (12 sts)
**Row 103** *K2tog* all stitches (6 sts)
**Row 105** K [add colour Y scrap yarn markers to the 2nd and 5th sts]
**Row 107** *Kfb* all stitches (12 sts)
**Row 109** *Kfb, K1* all stitches (18 sts)
**Row 111** *Kfb, K2* all stitches (24 sts)
**Row 113** K
**Row 115** K1, SKP, K18, K2tog, K1 (22 sts)
**Rows 117-124** Work in St st
**Row 125** K1, SKP, K16, K2tog, K1 (20 sts)
**Rows 127-130** Work in St st
**Row 131** K1, SKP, K14, K2tog, K1 (18 sts)
**Rows 133-136** Work in St st

# HALL OF FAME

*Bernard the Bison by Lottie*

**Who did you make it for?**
I made the project for my own home. Last year my boyfriend and I moved in together, and I thought this project would look great in our new living room.

**Where does it live?**
Bernard lives in our living room, right next to the window that gives a great view of the city centre of Amsterdam.

**What are you making at the moment?**
Besides knitting, I also love to sew. Currently, I'm sewing a few summer dresses. When it gets colder outside, I'll get back to knitting warm scarves and hats.

**WE'VE SELECTED SOME OF OUR FAVOURITE KNITTERS TO TELL US ABOUT THEIR SINCERELY LOUISE MAKES.**

**Who did you make it for?**
I knitted this project for my friend Milan and her daughter Vesper. Milan is a fan of everything girlie and pink, including unicorns. Seeing the pattern, I immediately knew it would make her very happy.

**Where does it live?**
My project is living in the East of the Netherlands now, near Arnhem. It was made in Utrecht, where I live.

**What are you making at the moment?**
I have about four WIPs at the moment. The Mae sweater, briochevron cowl, Marled Magic sweater and a garter stitch rug.

*Milan's Horse by Anouk*

*Mr Mallard by Sarah*

**Who did you make it for?**
Usually I do gift most of my knits but this one I loved too much to give away.

**Where does it live?**
He is hanging on the wall by the fireplace.

**What are you making at the moment?**
I am currently knitting the T-Rex trophy head for my nephew's birthday as he loves dinosaurs currently!

*Bear by Holly*

**Who did you make it for?**
I knitted the bear for my son Milo's first birthday present. He's a winter baby so it seemed like an apt choice. He loves lying on it and cuddling it!

**Where does it live?**
It's now living in his bedroom where it looks great!

**What are you making at the moment?**
I'm currently working on a corner-to-corner baby blanket for a friend who is expecting a baby, whilst also working on a crocheted cotton picnic blanket to use in the garden.

**Penguin Party Tea Set
by Joanne**

**Who did you make it for?**
No one specific. I'm the type of knitter who knits and then asks who wants it or waits for my friends to say 'I WANT IT!!!'

**Where does it live?**
It's actually living at work in the team room.

**What are you making at the moment?**
I'm currently working my way through my backlog of Curious Projects. I might need to quit my job and become a full time knitter so I can catch up.

**Moby by Sarah**

**Who did you make it for?**
I made it for myself, to have a very special Christmas scarf.

**Where does it live?**
It's living in Maastricht in the Netherlands, in a box, waiting for December to arrive. I'll wear it for the whole month and in January too!

**What are you making at the moment?**
I'm working on the latest Curious Project. I've never worked with raffia as wool before – very exciting! That's what I love so much – these Curious Projects make you use techniques and projects you'd never thought of using before.

**Loiuse the Rednose Reindeer
by Gaby**

**Who did you make it for?**
Me!

**Where does it live?**
He lives in the front room on top of the shelves I keep my yarn and unfinished projects in.

**What are you making at the moment?**
I'm currently working on many things. I've just started this month's Curious Project, have a 'Peaches' nearly finished for my niece's birthday next week, two jumpers and I also have bits of two Curious Projects I've not quite finished. And many, many more things in my head I want to start!

**Who did you make it for?**
I made the knit for myself! I've just moved to my flat up in Edinburgh and it was in dire need of some decorations to soften the place up. A big woolly sheep's head on the wall seemed like the perfect candidate!

**Where does it live?**
Caora hangs above my dining table, keeping me company at dinner time and eyeing up my salads.

**What are you making at the moment?**
I am soon to become Auntie to my 6th niece/nephew! I am planning to make matching animal hats for my four-year-old niece and her new baby sister, and maybe their mum and dad too. I'm still very much in the planning stages, but I think I might go with a fox theme as they're Londoners in an urban fox-heavy neighbourhood.

**Caora the Ram
by Bex**

**Beryl Bunny
by Heide**

**Who did you make it for?**
My six-month-old niece.

**Where does it live?**
South Africa.

**What are you making at the moment?**
A David Bowie lightning bolt sweater called Volt by Sue Stratford.

**Colin the Fox
by Lisa**

**Who did you make it for?**
Myself – it was my first scarf and the most labour intensive thing I've ever made!

**Where does it live?**
Colin lives on our hallway coat rack at the minute, although he has to hang up high as the cat is obsessed with him!

**What are you making at the moment?**
I'm working on the Coco sailor sweater by Wool and the Gang and the tiger scarf from Louise's HDIF collection.

**Ellis the Ram
by Sophie**

**Who did you make it for?**
It was my first knitting project and it was to decorate my new house.

**Where does it live?**
Living room wall – it's the faux taxidermy trophy wall. Quite a statement.

**What are you making at the moment?**
Crochet! Amigurumi dinosaurs for new babies.

# SINCERELY LOUISE TEAM MAKERS

**THE SINCERELY LOUISE TEAM HAVE BEEN BUSY KNITTING!**
Let's see what the Sincerely Louise team have been knitting. Our small team ranges from newbie knitters to crochet experts. They love crafting almost as much as I do!

**Bear Scarf
by Octavia**

**Jo and Joanna Bloggs Mice
by Eleanor**

**Triceratops
by Cara**

# Scrap Yarn Challenge

sincerelylouise
Porto Torres

Liked by **myhandmadeadventure**, **scarysjc** and **219 others**

**sincerelylouise** The scrap is back and live from Sardinia. I've snuck 25g of silver DK and 20g of purple DK yarn into my suitcase and need your help deciding what it should be made into. Just comment on this post to submit your idea and my favourite will be designed, knitted up and named after the person who suggested it. Oh and you'll win a copy of the pattern too. 🧶🧶🧶

View all 53 comments

On 8th August, on my summer holiday to Sardinia, I set a Scrap Yarn Challenge. I asked you what 25g (1oz) of silver DK yarn and 20g (¾oz) of purple DK yarn should be made into. I then chose my favourite suggestion and knitted it up. The winning idea has been named after the person who suggested it. Turn the page to see who's won!

# Roselle-Laura

Meet Roselle-Laura the Manta Ray! As you may know with previous Scrap Yarn Challenges, I've always been drawn to sea creatures. So, how could I resist this idea, especially as I was on holiday by the most beautiful coast I've ever been to.

Roselle submitted her idea on Instagram and Laura on Facebook, so credit has been given to both of them with this double-barrelled name.

## MATERIALS
**M** – Purple DK yarn x 20g (¾oz)
**C** – Silver DK yarn x 20g (¾oz)
4mm (US 6) straight needles, a couple of handfuls of toy stuffing, 2 x 10mm toy eyes and washers, black DK yarn for embroidery

## SCRAP YARN MAKERS
Colour **X** – Eye placement

# the Manta Ray

**BODY PIECES** - Make One in M and One in C
Cast on 6 stitches.
**Row 2** P all even rows unless otherwise stated. P rows have been <u>underlined</u>.
**Row 3** *Kfb* all stitches (12 sts)
**Row 5** *Kfb, K1* all stitches (18 sts)
**Row 7** K
**Row 9** K
<u>**Row 10**</u> P [add colour **X** scrap yarn markers to the 3rd and 16th of these sts]
**Row 11** Cast on 18 stitches at the beginning of the row. K all stitches (36 sts)
<u>**Row 12**</u> Cast on 18 stitches at the beginning of the row. P all stitches (54 sts)
**Row 13** K
**Row 15** K1, Kfb, K to the last three stitches, Kfb, K2 (56 sts)
**Row 17** K1, Kfb, K to the last three stitches, Kfb, K2 (58 sts)
**Row 19** K1, Kfb, K to the last three stitches, Kfb, K2 (60 sts)
**Row 21** K
**Row 23** K1, SKP, K to the last three stitches, K2tog, K1 (58 sts)
**Row 25** K1, SKP, K to the last three stitches, K2tog, K1 (56 sts)
**Row 27** Cast (bind) off 8 stitches, K to the end of the row (48 sts)
<u>**Row 28**</u> Cast (bind) off 8 stitches, P to the end of the row (40 sts)
**Row 29** K1, SKP, K3, SKP, K to the last eight stitches, K2tog, K3, K2tog, K1 (36 sts)
**Row 31** K1, SKP, K2, SKP, K to the last seven stitches, K2tog, K2, K2tog, K1 (32 sts)
**Row 33** K1, SKP, K1, SKP, K to the last six stitches, K2tog, K1, K2tog, K1 (28 sts)
**Row 35** K1, SKP, SKP, K to the last five stitches, K2tog, K2tog, K1 (24 sts)
**Row 37** K1, SKP, K to the last three stitches, K2tog, K1 (22 sts)
**Row 39** K
**Row 41** K1, SKP, K to the last three stitches, K2tog, K1 (20 sts)
**Row 43** K
**Row 45** K

**Row 47** K1, SKP, K to the last three stitches, K2tog, K1 (18 sts)
**Row 49** *K1, K2tog* all stitches (12 sts)
**Row 51** K1, SKP, K to the last three stitches, K2tog, K1 (10 sts)
**Row 53** K1, SKP, K to the last three stitches, K2tog, K1 (8 sts)
**Rows 55-82** Work in St st
**Row 83** K1, SKP, K2, K2tog, K1 (6 sts)
**Row 85** K
**Row 87** K1, SKP, K2tog, K1 (4 sts)
**Row 89** K
**Row 91** Cast (bind) off.

**CEPHALIC LOBE** - Make Two
Cast on 12 stitches in M.
**Row 2** P
**Rows 3-10** Work in St st
**Row 11** *K2tog* all stitches (6 sts)
Cut the yarn leaving a tail for sewing up. Thread it through the remaining six stitches and pull tightly. Then sew up from the thread-through end to the cast on edge using a mattress stitch. Leave the cast on edges open.

**SEWING UP**
Take the two body pieces and place the wrong sides together. Sew up using a mattress stitch in M, leaving a hole for stuffing. Lightly stuff the manta ray following the shape of the knit. Do not overstuff. Press the knit between your hands to flatten the stuffing. Stuff the cephalic lobes and place them onto the front of the manta ray, along the centre of the cast on edge seam. Leave a gap of 2cm (¾in) between them, then push them so they are facing downwards and sew into place. Place the 10mm toy eyes over the colour **X** scrap yarn markers. Remove the markers and secure the eyes with the washers. Sew up the hole in the body and weave in the loose ends. Embroider a small smile in between the lobes using some black DK yarn.

# GIANT ELEPHANT FAUX TAXIDERMY HEAD

For years and years I've been asked to design an elephant head. It's always been in the back of my mind and now I've finally got round to making one! As a child my favourite toy was an elephant, so in honour of him I'm calling this head Eddie.

**Materials**
Cygnet Seriously Chunky, 100% acrylic, 48m per 100g (52yd per 3½oz), or any super chunky (bulky) yarn
**M** - Slate Grey x 5 balls
**C** - Cream x 1 ball
DK yarn for sewing up, 200g (7oz) toy stuffing, 2 x 24mm toy eyes and washers, Sincerely Louise MDF backing board (see page 112), tiny amount of fishing line - 55lb

**Scrap Yarn Markers**
Colour W - Trunk placement
Colour X - Eye placement
Colour Y - Ear placement
Colour Z - Tusk placement

**Tension (Gauge):** 8 sts x 11 rows = 10cm (4in)

**Finished Size:** 57 x 36 x 58cm (22½ x 14 x 23in)

**TOP PIECE** – Make One
Cast on 5 stitches in M.
**Row 2** P all even rows.
**Row 3** *Kfb* all stitches (10 sts)
**Rows 5–28** Work in St st
**Row 29** K [add a colour W scrap yarn marker to the 5th of these sts]
**Row 31** K
**Row 33** K
**Row 35** K
**Row 37** K1, Kfb, K5, Kfb, K2 (12 sts)
**Row 39** K
**Row 41** K [add a colour W scrap yarn marker to the 6th of these sts]
**Row 43** K
**Row 45** K
**Row 47** *Kfb, K3* all stitches (15 sts)
**Row 49** K
**Row 51** *Kfb, K4* all stitches (18 sts)
**Row 53** K
**Row 55** *Kfb, K5* all stitches (21 sts)
**Row 57** K [add colour X scrap yarn markers to the 5th and 14th of these sts]
**Row 59** *Kfb, K6* all stitches (24 sts)
**Row 61** K
**Row 63** K
**Row 65** K
**Row 67** K [add colour Y scrap yarn markers to the 9th and 15th of these sts]
**Rows 69–76** Work in St st
**Row 77** *K6, K2tog* all stitches (21 sts)
**Row 79** *K5, K2tog* all stitches (18 sts)
**Row 81** *K4, K2tog* all stitches (15 sts)
**Row 83** K
**Row 85** Cast (bind) off loosely.

**UNDER PIECE** – Make One
Cast on 5 stitches in M.
**Row 2** P all even rows.
**Row 3** *Kfb* all stitches (10 sts)
**Row 5** K
**Row 7** [add a colour W scrap yarn marker to the 5th of these sts]
**Row 9** K
**Row 11** K
**Row 13** K
**Row 15** K [add a colour W scrap yarn marker to the 5th of these sts]
**Rows 17–36** Work in St st
**Row 37** K1, Kfb, K5, Kfb, K2 (12 sts)
**Rows 39–50** Work in St st
**Row 51** *Kfb, K3* all stitches (15 sts)
**Row 53** K [add colour Z scrap yarn markers to the 3rd, 6th, 10th and 13th of these sts]

**Row 55** K
**Row 57** K [add colour Z scrap yarn markers to the 3rd, 6th, 10th and 13th of these sts]
**Row 59** K
**Row 61** *Kfb, K4* all stitches (18 sts)
**Row 63** K
**Row 65** *Kfb, K5* all stitches (21 sts)
**Row 67** K [add colour Y scrap yarn markers to the 6th and 15th of these sts]
**Row 69** *Kfb, K6* all stitches (24 sts)
**Row 71** K
**Row 73** *Kfb, K7* all stitches (27 sts)
**Row 75** K
**Row 77** *Kfb, K8* all stitches (30 sts)
**Row 79** K
**Row 81** K
**Row 83** K
**Row 85** Cast (bind) off loosely.

**EARS** – Make Four Pieces
Cast on 15 stitches in M.
**Row 2** P all even rows.
**Row 3** *Kfb, K4* all stitches (18 sts)
**Row 5** *Kfb, K5* all stitches (21 sts)
**Row 7** K
**Row 9** *Kfb, K6* all stitches (24 sts)
**Rows 11–20** Work in St st
**Row 21** *K6, K2tog* all stitches (21 sts)
**Row 23** *K5, K2tog* all stitches (18 sts)
**Row 25** *K4, K2tog* all stitches (15 sts)
**Row 27** *K3, K2tog* all stitches (12 sts)
**Row 29** *K2, K2tog* all stitches (9 sts)
**Row 31** Cast (bind) off.

**TUSKS** – Make Two
Cast on 12 stitches in C.
**Row 2** P all even rows.
**Rows 3–14** Work in St st
**Row 15** *K2, K2tog* all stitches (9 sts)
**Row 17** K
**Row 19** *K1, K2tog* all stitches (6 sts)
**Row 21** *K2tog* all stitches (3 sts)
Cut the yarn leaving a tail for sewing up. Thread it through the remaining three stitches and pull tightly. Sew from the thread-through end to the cast on edge using a mattress stitch. Leave the cast on edges open. Lightly stuff each tusk.

**SEWING UP**
Weave in the loose ends. Take the top and under pieces of the head and place the wrong sides together. Sew from

the cast (bound) off edge to the cast on edge using a mattress stitch in M. Sew along the cast on edge and up the other side to the cast (bound) off edge. Leave the cast (bound) off edges open.

**The Eyes**
Place the toy eyes over the colour X scrap yarn markers. Remove the markers and secure the eyes with washers.

**The Ears**
Take two ear pieces and place the wrong sides together. Sew up using a mattress stitch in M, leaving the cast on edges open. Repeat for the second ear. Do not stuff the ears. Place the first ear between the colour Y scrap yarn markers on the right-hand side of the head. Sew the cast on edges of the ear against the knit of the head using M. Repeat for the second ear, placing it between the left-hand set of markers. Remove the markers.

**The Tusks**
Place one tusk between the right-hand set of colour Z scrap yarn markers on the under piece of the head. Sew the cast on edge of the tusk against the head of the knit using C. Repeat for the second tusk, placing it between the left-hand set of markers and sew into place. Remove the markers.

**The Trunk**
Find the set of colour W scrap yarn markers on the top piece. They will be in the centre of the trunk with several rows between them. Thread some M yarn and secure it into the head, where one of the markers is. Sew the yarn from this marker to the next colour W marker and pull tightly. This will bunch up the stitches and pull the trunk together. Sew back into the first marker and then out again into the second, pulling tightly. Repeat this process several times until the trunk is secure.

Repeat this technique at the other set of colour W scrap yarn markers on the under piece. This will pull the end of the trunk slightly forwards. Remove the markers and weave in the loose ends.

# MOUNTING YOUR ELEPHANT HEAD

The super chunky (bulky) animal head fits perfectly onto the Sincerely Louise MDF backing board. This technique has been demonstrated here on a fawn head with black DK yarn. For your animal head, use the corresponding coloured DK sewing up yarn.

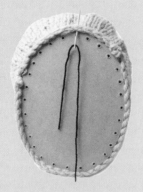

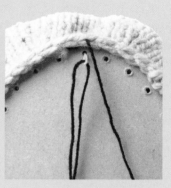

**1**. Take the board and place it inside the head. Thread a sewing needle with the DK yarn and tie a knot at one end.

**2**. Sew into the centre of the cast (bound) off edge. Insert the needle close to the first point it was sewn into and pull through.

**3**. Sew into the hole below where the needle just exited the cast (bound) off edge.

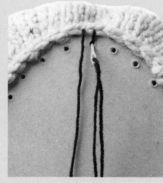

**4**. Push the needle through the hole and three rows into the back of the head.

**5**. Sew back into the cast (bound) off edge, left of the sewn hole.

**6**. Repeat step 4 into this same hole to create a V shape, but insert the needle diagonally to the left, so that it exits between two holes.

**7**. Sew back into the cast (bound) off edge, between the two holes, then insert into the next hole. Sew into the cast (bound) off edge to the left. Sew back into the same hole, creating a V shape.

**8**. Repeat ¾ of the way around the head. Add any extra stuffing to the chin and sew up the rest of the head. Then sew in reverse, working anticlockwise around the board. Sew the fishing line into the top loop, securing it with a knot. Weave in loose ends.

# Knitter's Homework

Solve the equations by finding the number of stitches.

Kfb, K9, SKP, K20, Kfb, K1 = (   sts)

K1M, Kfb in M, K4M, K7C, K4M, Kfb in M, K2M = (   sts)

*P8, K3* seven times, P8 = (   sts)

K1, SKP, K47, Cast (bind) off 10 stitches, K47, K2tog, K1 = (   sts)

K14C, K8M, K19C, K17M, K2tog in M, K19M = (   sts)

*K5, K2tog* six times = (   sts)

K8, L31, K5, L42, K8 = (   sts)

K40M, K7C, K11B, K55M, K8C, K30M = (   sts)

K1, SKP, SKP, Kfb, K39, Kfb, SKP, SKP, K1 = (   sts)

K11, Kfb, K1, Kfb, K12 = (   sts)

Answers on page 111

# Crocodile Rug

### MATERIALS
Bobbiny 5mm Premium Cord, 100m per 500g
(109yd per 17½oz), or any corded yarn
**M** – Eucalyptus Green x 6 balls
9mm (US 13) 120cm (48in) circular needles
(don't panic: this project is knitted straight on the
circular needles), stitch holder,
150g (5oz) toy stuffing,
2 x 24mm toy eyes and washers,
black super chunky (bulky) yarn for embroidery

### TENSION (GAUGE)
8 sts x 12 rows = 10cm (4in)

### FINISHED SIZE
180 x 70 x 5cm (71 x 27½ x 2in)

**TOP PIECE** – Make One
Cast on 6 stitches in M. Use the circular needles throughout this project. Use them like straight needles. The cord is big enough for all the stitches and will take the weight of the knitting.

**Row 2** P all even rows until otherwise stated. P rows from Rows 2–62 have been <u>underlined</u>.

**Row 3** *Kfb, K1* all stitches (9 sts)
**Row 5** *Kfb, K2 * all stitches (12 sts)
**Row 7** K
**Row 9** K
**Row 11** K
**Row 13** K1, SKP, K6, K2tog, K1 (10 sts)
**Row 15** Kfb, SKP, K4, K2tog, Kfb (10 sts)
**Row 17** K
**Row 19** K

**Row 21** Kfb, K to the last two stitches, Kfb, K1 (12 sts)
**Row 23** K
**Row 25** K
**Row 27** Kfb, K to the last two stitches, Kfb, K1 (14 sts)
**Row 29** K
**Row 31** K
**Row 33** Kfb, K to the last two stitches, Kfb, K1 (16 sts)

**Row 35** K

**Row 37** K

**Row 39** Kfb, K to the last two stitches, Kfb, K1 (18 sts)

**Row 41** The crocodile's eyes use the wrap around technique. Here's how to do it:

K2 *(Knit two stitches as per usual.)*

K5, WA, TURN *(Knit another five stitches, then bring the yarn forwards between the two needles. It will now be between the stitch just worked and the next stitch on the left-hand needle. Slip the next stitch across from the left-hand needle to the right-hand needle. The yarn will still be between these two stitches and at the front of the work. Then wrap the yarn around the front of the slipped stitch and place the yarn back between the two needles, so it is now at the back of the work. Slip the stitch back onto the left-hand needle. The yarn will be between the slipped stitch and the unworked stitch next to it. Turn the work so the wrong side is facing you.)*

P5, WA, TURN *(Purl five stitches, then take the yarn and place it between the two needles, so it is at the back of the work (from the wrong side's perspective). It will once again be between the stitch just worked and the one ready to be worked. Slip the next stitch on the purl row onto the right-hand needle. The yarn will be between these two stitches. Bring the yarn back between the needles so it is now at the front of the work. It will have wrapped around the slipped stitch. Slip the stitch back onto the left-hand needle. The yarn will be between the slipped stitch and the unworked stitch next to it. Turn the work.)*

K5, WA, TURN *(Knit five stitches. These are the five stitches you have just knitted, wrapped around, purled and wrapped again. Now continue the pattern, wrapping and turning as described in the above steps.)*

P5, WA, TURN

K5, WA, TURN

P5, WA, TURN

K9 *(Knit nine stitches. There will now be 11 stitches on the right-hand needle, completing the first eye. You will now start making the second eye with the next five stitches on the left-hand needle.)*

K5, WA, TURN

P5, WA, TURN

K5, WA, TURN

P5, WA, TURN

K5, WA, TURN

P5, WA, TURN

K7 *(Knit the five stitches of the eye plus the final two stitches on the left-hand needle. You will now have 18 stitches on the right-hand needle.)*

**Row 42** P all stitches

**Row 43** Kfb, K to the last two stitches, Kfb, K1 (20 sts)

**Row 45** K

**Row 47** K

**Row 49** Kfb, K5, K2tog, K2, K2tog, K2, K2tog, K2, Kfb, K1 (19 sts)

**Row 51** Kfb, K5, K2tog, K1, K2tog, K1, K2tog, K3, Kfb, K1 (18 sts)

**Row 53** Kfb, Kfb, K4, K2tog, K2tog, K2tog, K3, Kfb, Kfb, K1 (19 sts)

**Row 55** K1, Kfbf, Kfbf, K to the last four stitches, Kfbf, Kfbf, K2 (27 sts)

**Row 57** Cast on 5 stitches, K to the end of the row (32 sts)

**Row 58** Cast on 5 stitches, P to the end of the row (37 sts)

**Row 59** K1, Kfbf, Kfbf, K to the last four stitches, Kfbf, Kfbf, K2 (45 sts)

**Row 61** Cast on 6 stitches, K to the end of the row (51 sts)

**Row 62** Cast on 6 stitches, P to the end of the row (57 sts)

**Row 63** K1, Kfb, K to the last three stitches, Kfb, K2 (59 sts)

**Rows 65–70** Work in St st

**Row 71** K1, SKP, K to the last three stitches, K2tog, K1 (57 sts)

**Row 73** Cast (bind) off 18 stitches, K to the end of the row (39 sts)

**Row 74** Cast (bind) off 18 stitches, P to the end of the row (21 sts)

**Row 75** K1, Kfb, K4, P3, K3, P3, K3, Kfb, K2 (23 sts)

**Row 76** P7, K3, P3, K3, P7

**Row 77** K7, P3, K3, P3, K7

**Row 78** P7, K3, P3, K3, P7

**Row 79** K1, Kfb, K to the last three stitches, Kfb, K2 (25 sts)

**Row 80** P

**Row 81** K

**Row 82** P

**Row 83** K1, Kfb, K6, P3, K3, P3, K5, Kfb, K2 (27 sts)

**Row 84** P9, K3, P3, K3, P9

**Row 85** K9, P3, K3, P3, K9

**Row 86** P9, K3, P3, K3, P9

**Row 87** K

**Row 88** P

**Row 89** K1, Kfb, K to the last three stitches, Kfb, K2 (29 sts)

**Row 90** P

**Row 91** K4, P3, K3, P3, K3, P3, K3, P3, K4

**Row 92** P4, K3, P3, K3, P3, K3, P3, K3, P4

**Row 93** K4, P3, K3, P3, K3, P3, K3, P3, K4

**Row 94** P4, K3, P3, K3, P3, K3, P3, K3, P4

**Row 95** K

**Row 96** P

**Row 97** K1, Kfb, K to the last three stitches, Kfb, K2 (31 sts)

**Row 98** P

**Row 99** K5, P3, K3, P3, K3, P3, K3, P3, K5

**Row 100** P5, K3, P3, K3, P3, K3, P3, K3, P5

**Row 101** K5, P3, K3, P3, K3, P3, K3, P3, K5

**Row 102** P5, K3, P3, K3, P3, K3, P3, K3, P5

**Row 103** K

**Row 104** P

**Row 105** K

**Row 106** P

**Row 107** K5, P3, K3, P3, K3, P3, K3, P3, K5

**Row 108** P5, K3, P3, K3, P3, K3, P3, K3, P5

**Row 109** K5, P3, K3, P3, K3, P3, K3, P3, K5

**Row 110** P5, K3, P3, K3, P3, K3, P3, K3, P5

**Row 111** K1, SKP, K to the last three stitches, K2tog, K1 (29 sts)

**Row 112** P

**Row 113** K1, SKP, K to the last three stitches, K2tog, K1 (27 sts)

**Row 114** P

**Row 115** K1, Kfb, K1, P3, K3, P3, K3, P3, K3, P3, Kfb, K2 (29 sts)

**Row 116** P4, K3, P3, K3, P3, K3, P3, K3, P4

**Row 117** K1, Kfb, K2, P3, K3, P3, K3, P3, K3, P3, K1, Kfb, K2 (31 sts)

**Row 118** P5, K3, P3, K3, P3, K3, P3, K3, P5

**Row 119** K1, Kfb, Kfb, K to the last four stitches, Kfb, Kfb, K2 (35 sts)

**Row 120** P

**Row 121** K1, Kfb, Kfb, K to the last four stitches, Kfb, Kfb, K2 (39 sts)

**Row 122** P

**Row 123** K1, Kfb, Kfb, K6, P3, K3, P3, K3, P3, K3, P3, K5, Kfb, Kfb, K2 (43 sts)

**Row 124** P11, K3, P3, K3, P3, K3, P3, K3, P11

**Row 125** K1, Kfb, Kfb, K8, P3, K3, P3, K3, P3, K3, P3, K7, Kfb, Kfb, K2 (47 sts)

**Row 126** P13, K3, P3, K3, P3, K3, P3, K3, P13

**Row 127** K1, Kfb, K to the last three stitches, Kfb, K2 (49 sts)

**Row 128** P

**Row 129** K1, Kfb, K to the last three stitches, Kfb, K2 (51 sts)

**Row 130** P

**Row 131** K12, Kfb, K2, P3, K3, P3, K3, P3, K3, P3, K1, Kfb, K13 (53 sts)

**Row 132** P16, K3, P3, K3, P3, K3, P3, K3, P16

**Row 133** K16, P3, K3, P3, K3, P3, K3, P3, K16

**Row 134** P16, K3, P3, K3, P3, K3, P3, K3, P16

*Right Leg*

**Row 135** K1, Kfb, K10 (13 sts), TURN, placing the remaining 41 stitches on a holder to be worked later.

**Row 136** P the 13 stitches

**Row 137** K10, K2tog, K1 (12 sts)

**Row 138** P all even rows from here.

**Row 139** K1, Kfb, K7, K2tog, K1 (12 sts)

**Row 141** K9, K2tog, K1 (11 sts)

**Row 143** K1, Kfb, K6, K2tog, K1 (11 sts)

**Row 145** K8, K2tog, K1 (10 sts)

**Row 147** K

**Row 149** K

**Row 151** K

**Row 153** K1, SKP, K4, K2tog, K1 (8 sts)

**Row 155** K1, SKP, K2, K2tog, K1 (6 sts)

**Row 157** Cast (bind) off.

*Left Leg*

Move the 41 stitches from the holder onto the left-hand needle ready to be worked from Row 135.

**Row 135** Reattach the yarn and K to the last three stitches, Kfb, K2 (42 sts)

**Row 136** P13, TURN, placing the remaining 29 stitches on a holder to be worked later.

**Row 137** K1, SKP, K10 (12 sts)

**Row 138** P all even rows from here.

**Row 139** K1, SKP, K6, Kfb, K2 (12 sts)

**Row 141** K1, SKP, K9 (11 sts)

**Row 143** K1, SKP, K5, Kfb, K2 (11 sts)

**Row 145** K1, SKP, K8 (10 sts)

**Row 147** K

**Row 149** K

**Row 151** K

**Row 153** K1, SKP, K4, K2tog, K1 (8 sts)

**Row 155** K1, SKP, K2, K2tog, K1 (6 sts)

**Row 157** Cast (bind) off.

*Tail*

Move the 29 stitches from the holder onto the left-hand needle ready to be worked from Row 136.

**Row 136** Reattach the yarn and P all stitches

**Row 137** K1, SKP, K to the last three stitches, K2tog, K1 (27 sts)

**Row 138** P

**Row 139** K1, SKP, P3, K3, P3, K3, P3, K3, P3, K2tog, K1 (25 sts)

**Row 140** P2, K3, P3, K3, P3, K3, P3, K3, P2

**Row 141** K2, P3, K3, P3, K3, P3, K3, P3, K2

**Row 142** P2, K3, P3, K3, P3, K3, P3, K3, P2

**Row 143** K1, SKP, K to the last three stitches, K2tog, K1 (23 sts)

**Row 144** P

**Row 145** K

**Row 146** P

**Row 147** K2, P2, K3, P3, K3, P3, K3, P2, K2

**Row 148** P2, K2, P3, K3, P3, K3, P3, K2, P2

**Row 149** K2, P2, K3, P3, K3, P3, K3, P2, K2

**Row 150** P2, K2, P3, K3, P3, K3, P3, K2, P2

**Row 151** K1, SKP, K to the last three stitches, K2tog, K1 (21 sts)

**Row 152** P

**Row 153** K

**Row 154** P

**Row 155** K2, P1, K3, P3, K3, P3, K3, P1, K2

**Row 156** P2, K1, P3, K3, P3, K3, P3, K1, P2

**Row 157** K2, P1, K3, P3, K3, P3, K3, P1, K2

**Row 158** P2, K1, P3, K3, P3, K3, P3, K1, P2

**Row 159** K1, SKP, K to the last three stitches, K2tog, K1 (19 sts)

**Row 160** P

**Row 161** K

**Row 162** P

**Row 163** K5, P3, K3, P3, K5

**Row 164** P5, K3, P3, K3, P5

**Row 165** K5, P3, K3, P3, K5

**Row 166** P5, K3, P3, K3, P5

**Row 167** K1, SKP, K to the last three stitches, K2tog, K1 (17 sts)

**Row 168** P

**Row 169** K

**Row 170** P

**Row 171** K4, P3, K3, P3, K4

**Row 172** P4, K3, P3, K3, P4

**Row 173** K4, P3, K3, P3, K4

**Row 174** P4, K3, P3, K3, P4

**Row 175** K1, SKP, K to the last three stitches, K2tog, K1 (15 sts)

**Row 176** P

**Row 177** K

**Row 178** P

**Row 179** K3, P3, K3, P3, K3

**Row 180** P3, K3, P3, K3, P3

**Row 181** K3, P3, K3, P3, K3

**Row 182** P3, K3, P3, K3, P3

**Row 183** K1, SKP, K to the last three stitches, K2tog, K1 (13 sts)

**Row 184** P

**Row 185** K

**Row 186** P

**Row 187** K2, P3, K3, P3, K2

**Row 188** P2, K3, P3, K3, P2

**Row 189** K2, P3, K3, P3, K2

**Row 190** P2, K3, P3, K3, P2

**Row 191** K6, K2tog, K5 (12 sts)

**Row 192** P

**Row 193** K

**Row 194** P

**Row 195** K2, P3, K2, P3, K2

**Row 196** P2, K3, P2, K3, P2

**Row 197** K2, P3, K2, P3, K2

**Row 198** P2, K3, P2, K3, P2

**Row 199** K1, SKP, K to the last three stitches, K2tog, K1 (10 sts)

**Row 200** P

**Row 201** K

**Row 202** P

**Row 203** K2, P2, K2, P2, K2

**Row 204** P2, K2, P2, K2, P2

**Row 205** K
**Row 206** P
**Row 207** K1, SKP, K4, K2tog, K1 (8 sts)
**Row 208** P
**Row 209** K2, P1, K2, P1, K2
**Row 210** P2, K1, P2, K1, P2
**Row 211** K1, SKP, K2, K2tog, K1 (6 sts)
**Row 212** P
**Row 213** K
**Row 214** P
**Row 215** K1, SKP, K2tog, K1 (4 sts)
**Row 216** P
**Row 217** K
**Row 218** P
**Row 219** Cast (bind) off.

**UNDER PIECE** – Make One
Cast on 6 stitches in M.
Row 2 P all even rows unless otherwise stated. P rows have been underlined.
**Row 3** *Kfb, K1* all stitches (9 sts)
**Row 5** *Kfb, K2 * all stitches (12 sts)
**Row 7** K
**Row 9** K
**Row 11** K
**Row 13** K1, SKP, K6, K2tog, K1 (10 sts)
**Row 15** Kfb, SKP, K4, K2tog, Kfb (10 sts)
**Row 17** K
**Row 19** K
**Row 21** Kfb, K to the last two stitches, Kfb, K1 (12 sts)
**Row 23** K
**Row 25** K
**Row 27** Kfb, K to the last two stitches, Kfb, K1 (14 sts)
**Row 29** K
**Row 31** K
**Row 33** Kfb, K to the last two stitches, Kfb, K1 (16 sts)
**Row 35** K
**Row 37** K
**Row 39** Kfb, K to the last two stitches, Kfb, K1 (18 sts)
**Row 41** K
**Row 43** Kfb, K to the last two stitches, Kfb, K1 (20 sts)
**Row 45** K
**Row 47** K
**Row 49** Kfb, K5, K2tog, K2, K2tog, K2, K2tog, K2, Kfb, K1 (19 sts)

**Row 51** Kfb, K5, K2tog, K1, K2tog, K1, K2tog, K3, Kfb, K1 (18 sts)
**Row 53** Kfb, Kfb, K4, K2tog, K2tog, K2tog, K3, Kfb, Kfb, K1 (19 sts)
**Row 55** K1, Kfbf, Kfbf, K to the last four stitches, Kfbf, Kfbf, K2 (27 sts)
**Row 57** Cast on 5 stitches, K to the end of the row (32 sts)
**Row 58** Cast on 5 stitches, P to the end of the row (37 sts)
**Row 59** K1, Kfbf, Kfbf, K to the last four stitches, Kfbf, Kfbf, K2 (45 sts)
**Row 61** Cast on 6 stitches, K to the end of the row (51 sts)
**Row 62** Cast on 6 stitches, P to the end of the row (57 sts)
**Row 63** K1, Kfb, K to the last three stitches, Kfb, K2 (59 sts)
**Row 65** K
**Row 67** K
**Row 69** K
**Row 71** K1, SKP, K to the last three stitches, K2tog, K1 (57 sts)
**Row 73** Cast (bind) off 18 stitches, K to the end of the row (39 sts)
**Row 74** Cast (bind) off 18 stitches, P to the end of the row (21 sts)
**Row 75** K1, Kfb, K to the last three stitches, Kfb, K2 (23 sts)
**Row 77** K
**Row 79** K1, Kfb, K to the last three stitches, Kfb, K2 (25 sts)
**Row 81** K
**Row 83** K1, Kfb, K to the last three stitches, Kfb, K2 (27 sts)
**Row 85** K
**Row 87** K
**Row 89** K1, Kfb, K to the last three stitches, Kfb, K2 (29 sts)
**Row 91** K
**Row 93** K
**Row 95** K
**Row 97** K1, Kfb, K to the last three stitches, Kfb, K2 (31 sts)
**Row 99** K
**Row 101** K
**Row 103** K
**Row 105** K
**Row 107** K
**Row 109** K
**Row 111** K1, SKP, K to the last three stitches, K2tog, K1 (29 sts)
**Row 113** K1, SKP, K to the last three stitches, K2tog, K1 (27 sts)

**Row 115** K1, Kfb, K to the last three stitches, Kfb, K2 (29 sts)
**Row 117** K1, Kfb, K to the last three stitches, Kfb, K2 (31 sts)
**Row 119** K1, Kfb, Kfb, K to the last four stitches, Kfb, Kfb, K2 (35 sts)
**Row 121** K1, Kfb, Kfb, K to the last four stitches, Kfb, Kfb, K2 (39 sts)
**Row 123** K1, Kfb, Kfb, K to the last four stitches, Kfb, Kfb, K2 (43 sts)
**Row 125** K1, Kfb, Kfb, K to the last four stitches, Kfb, Kfb, K2 (47 sts)
**Row 127** K1, Kfb, K to the last three stitches, Kfb, K2 (49 sts)
**Row 129** K1, Kfb, K to the last three stitches, Kfb, K2 (51 sts)
**Row 131** K1, Kfb, K to the last three stitches, Kfb, K2 (53 sts)
**Row 133** K

*Right Leg*
**Row 135** K1, Kfb, K10 (13 sts), TURN, placing the remaining 41 stitches on a holder to be worked later.
**Row 136** P the 13 stitches
**Row 137** K10, K2tog, K1 (12 sts)
**Row 139** K1, Kfb, K7, K2tog, K1 (12 sts)
**Row 141** K9, K2tog, K1 (11 sts)
**Row 143** K1, Kfb, K6, K2tog, K1 (11 sts)
**Row 145** K8, K2tog, K1 (10 sts)
**Row 147** K
**Row 149** K
**Row 151** K
**Row 153** K1, SKP, K4, K2tog, K1 (8 sts)
**Row 155** K1, SKP, K2, K2tog, K1 (6 sts)
**Row 157** Cast (bind) off.

*Left Leg*
Move the 41 stitches from the holder onto the left-hand needle ready to be worked from Row 135.
**Row 135** Reattach the yarn and K to the last three stitches, Kfb, K2 (42 sts)
**Row 136** P13, TURN, placing the remaining 29 stitches on a holder to be worked later.
**Row 137** K1, SKP, K10 (12 sts)
**Row 139** K1, SKP, K6, Kfb, K2 (12 sts)
**Row 141** K1, SKP, K9 (11 sts)
**Row 143** K1, SKP, K5, Kfb, K2 (11 sts)

**Row 145** K1, SKP, K8 (10 sts)
**Row 147** K
**Row 149** K
**Row 151** K
**Row 153** K1, SKP, K4, K2tog, K1 (8 sts)
**Row 155** K1, SKP, K2, K2tog, K1 (6 sts)
**Row 157** Cast (bind) off.

*Tail*
Move the 29 stitches from the holder onto the left-hand needle ready to be worked from Row 136.
**Row 136** Reattach the yarn and P all stitches
**Row 137** K1, SKP, K to the last three stitches, K2tog, K1 (27 sts)
**Row 139** K1, SKP, K to the last three stitches, K2tog, K1 (25 sts)
**Row 141** K
**Row 143** K1, SKP, K to the last three stitches, K2tog, K1 (23 sts)
**Row 145** K
**Row 147** K
**Row 149** K
**Row 151** K1, SKP, K to the last three stitches, K2tog, K1 (21 sts)
**Row 153** K

**Row 155** K
**Row 157** K
**Row 159** K1, SKP, K to the last three stitches, K2tog, K1 (19 sts)
**Row 161** K
**Row 163** K
**Row 165** K
**Row 167** K1, SKP, K to the last three stitches, K2tog, K1 (17 sts)
**Row 169** K
**Row 171** K
**Row 173** K
**Row 175** K1, SKP, K to the last three stitches, K2tog, K1 (15 sts)
**Row 177** K
**Row 179** K
**Row 181** K
**Row 183** K1, SKP, K to the last three stitches, K2tog, K1 (13 sts)
**Row 185** K
**Row 187** K
**Row 189** K
**Row 191** K6, K2tog, K5 (12 sts)
**Row 193** K
**Row 195** K
**Row 197** K1, SKP, K to the last three stitches, K2tog, K1 (10 sts)

**Row 199** K
**Row 201** K
**Row 203** K
**Row 205** K1, SKP, K4 K2tog, K1 (8 sts)
**Row 207** K
**Row 209** K1, SKP, K2, K2tog, K1 (6 sts)
**Row 211** K
**Row 213** K1, SKP, K2tog, K1 (4 sts)
**Row 215** K
**Row 217** Cast (bind) off.

# Sewing Up

Weave in the loose ends. Take the top and under pieces and place the wrong sides together. Sew up using a mattress stitch in M, leaving a hole for stuffing. Plump up the toy stuffing and stuff the head, following the shape of the knit. Add a very small amount of stuffing to each leg, but do not stuff the body and tail. Take the 24mm toy eyes and place each one in the centre of the bumps on the top of the head, created by the wrap arounds and short rows. Secure the eyes with washers and sew up the hole in the body. Weave in the loose ends.

Using the black super chunky (bulky) wool, embroider the nostrils onto the crocodile's snout. Embroider two 3cm (1in) vertical lines from the cast on edge seam, leaving a gap of 4cm (1½cm) between them. Repeat this several times, until each nostril measures 2cm (¾in) in width. Weave in the loose ends.

World

# Map of Faux Taxidermists

This is the army of Sincerely Louise knitters. Crafters all over the world have faux taxidermy all over their walls. Can you see your pin on the map?

# QUIZ ANSWERS

## ROUND ONE

Fisherman's Rib – Brioche

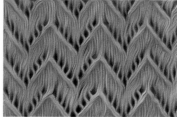

Chevron Lace

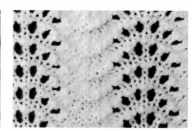

Feather and Fan

Garter Stitch

Lattice with Moss (Seed) Stitch

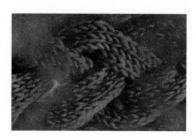

Cable

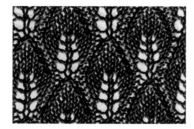

Leaf Stitch

Moss (Seed) Stitch

Waffle Stitch

## ROUND TWO

1. DPNs
2. Stocking (stockinette) stitch
3. 4mm
4. Knitting and watching Netflix
5. Worsted
6. Royal Albert Hall
7. Second Sock Syndrome
8. Amigurumi
9. Fair Isle
10. 55 calories

## ROUND THREE

1. Westknits
2. Sue Stratford
3. King Cole
4. Janie Crow
5. Kaffe Fassett
6. Kerry Lord
7. Stephanie Dosen
8. Coop Knits – Rachel Coopey
9. Erika Knight
10. Dedri Uys

## ROUND FOUR

1. Shreddies
2. *The Clangers*
3. Ron Weasley
4. Dr Who
5. *Gilmore Girls*
6. Gromit
7. Miss Marple
8. *What We Do in the Shadows*
9. *Black Panther*
10. *Friends*

## ROUND FIVE

**1.** 'Where's Me Jumper'
The Sultans of Ping FC

**2.** 'Season Of The Witch'
Donovan

**3.** 'Dress Up In You'
Belle and Sebastian

**4.** 'Don't Marry Her'
The Beautiful South

**5.** 'You Spin Me Round'
Dead or Alive

**6.** 'Rip It Up'
Orange Juice

**7.** 'Unravel'
Björk

**8.** 'Wonderwall'
Oasis

**9.** 'Diamonds And Pearls'
Prince

**10.** 'I'm Going Slightly Mad'
Queen

## ROUND SIX

**1.** Ryan Gosling

**2.** Krysten Ritter

**3.** Julia Roberts

**4.** Jenny Eclair

**5.** Sarah Jessica Parker

**6.** Uma Thurman

**7.** Russel Crowe

**8.** Catherine Zeta Jones

**9.** Audrey Hepburn

**10.** Christina Hendricks

## BONUS QUESTIONS

**1.** 1589

**2.** Lace
Fingering
Sock
4ply (sport)
DK
Aran (worsted)
Chunky (bulky)
Super chunky (bulky)

**3.** 22 shades

# FIND THE FIBRE

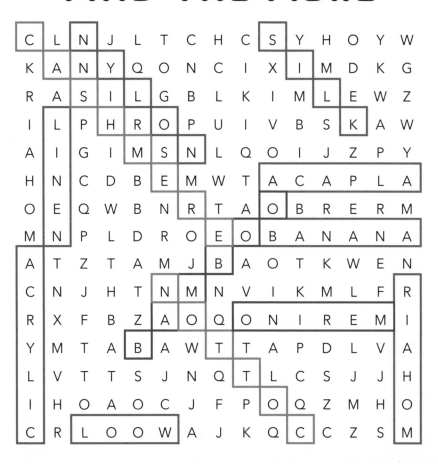

109

# CRAFTY CROSSWORD

**Across / Down grid:**

1. MAGICLOOP (down)
2. RAVELLY (down)
3. TUNISIAN (across) / TOTTOSESHELL (down)
4. FRENCH (across)
5. RIBSTITCH (across)
6. SLIPPED (across) / SCHEEREEJES (down)
7. CASHMERE (across)
8. ALLYPALLY (across)
9. YARNCAKE (down)

## FIND THE
### ODD BALL OUT

## At The Craft Fair

1. How many balls of wool are there?
   104

2. How many people are knitting?
   Three people are knitting

3. Who's won first prize?
   A chihuahua in a knitted coat

4. What shoes is Louise wearing?
   Dr. Martens

5. How many animals are at the fair?
   Four - one dog and three animal heads

# Knitter's Homework

Kfb, K9, SKP, K20, Kfb, K1 = (35 sts)

K1M, Kfb in M, K4M, K7C, K4M, Kfb in M, K2M = (22 sts)

*P8, K3* seven times, P8 = (85 sts)

K1, SKP, K47, Cast (bind) off 10 stitches, K47, K2tog, K1 = (89 sts)

K14C, K8M, K19C, K17M, K2tog in M, K19M = (78 sts)

*K5, K2tog* six times = (36 sts)

K8, L31, K5, L42, K8 = (94 sts)

K40M, K7C, K11B, K55M, K8C, K30M = (151 sts)

K1, SKP, SKP, Kfb, K39, Kfb, SKP, SKP, K1 = (49 sts)

K11, Kfb, K1, Kfb, K12 = (28 sts)

## About the Author

Louise Walker is an award-winning knitting pattern designer with a degree in commercial photography. After launching Sincerely Louise in 2014, her work has been featured in national and international press. Louise has collaborated with the likes of Boden, the V&A, Mollie Makes and Innocent Smoothies.

Now based in Sheffield, UK, next to Bramall Lane (go Blades), Louise and her partner Peter run their small businesses from the top floor of an old cutlery factory. Louise spends her time knitting and watching terrible reality television shows.

This book is dedicated to Peter Butler. Words cannot describe how amazing he is. Without his continued love and support this book would not exist and it certainly would not be aligned to any kind of baseline grid.

## Suppliers

### Sincerely Louise
Wool, kits and mounting boards
www.sincerelylouise.co.uk

## Yarn

### Bobbiny
www.bobbiny.com

### Cygnet Yarns Ltd
www.cygnetyarns.com
Also available internationally from www.deramores.com

### Rico Design
www.rico-design.de
Also available from all good online retailers

### Scheepjes
www.scheepjes.com
Also available from all good online retailers

### Stylecraft
www.stylecraft-yarns.co.uk
Also available from all good online retailers

### Yarn Stories
www.yarnstories.com
Also available internationally from www.loveknitting.com

## PAVILION

Whatever the craft, we have the book for you – just head straight to Pavilion's crafty headquarters.

Pavilion Craft is the one-stop destination for all our fabulous craft books. Sign up for our regular newsletters and follow us on social media to receive updates on new books, competitions and interviews with our bestselling authors.

We look forward to meeting you!

www.pavilionbooks.com/craft